D0327082

Welcome to the Poisoned Chalice

Welcome to the Poisoned Chalice

The Destruction of Greece and the Future of Europe

JAMES K. GALBRAITH

Yale UNIVERSITY PRESS

New Haven & London

Yale University Press books may be purchased in quantity for educational,
business, or promotional use. For information, please e-mail
sales.press@yale.edu (U.S. office) or sales@yaleup.co.uk (U.K. office).

Set in Janson type by Integrated Publishing Solutions,
Grand Rapids, Michigan.
Printed in the United States of America.

Library of Congress Control Number: 2015955723
ISBN 978-0-300-22044-5 (cloth : alk. paper)

A catalogue record for this book is available from the British Library.

This paper meets the requirements of ANSI/NISO Z39.48-1992
(Permanence of Paper).

10 9 8 7 6 5 4 3 2 1

The bankruptcy and decay of Europe, if we allow it to proceed, will affect everyone in the long run.

—John Maynard Keynes, 1919

Contents

ONE
Welcome to the Poisoned Chalice   1

PART I 2010–2014

TWO
Europe's Crisis:
Thinking It Through to the End   23

THREE
Greece and the European Project   28

FOUR
A Question of Moral Responsibility   31

FIVE
Neither Austerity nor Growth:
Solidarity *Is Europe's Only Hope*   36

Contents

SIX

The Victory of SYRIZA Is Not Against American
Interests *with Yanis Varoufakis* 39

SEVEN

The United States and Europe:
What Is Going On? 42

PART II 2015

EIGHT

The Greek Hope 49

NINE

A Message to Sarah Raskin 52

TEN

A Comment on the Way Forward 56

ELEVEN

America Must Rally to Greece 58

TWELVE

Reading the Greek Deal Correctly 61

THIRTEEN

A Great German Greek Grexit Game? 66

FOURTEEN

The Political Level 70

FIFTEEN

A Report from Athens 73

Contents

SIXTEEN
Does Europe Need Debt Relief?   81

SEVENTEEN
Long-Term Strategy Through a Realistic Lens   83

EIGHTEEN
Strategic Options   91

NINETEEN
A Further Message to Sarah Raskin   94

TWENTY
The Greek Drama and Democracy in Europe   97

TWENTY-ONE
Notes on the Meeting, Varoufakis-Schäuble, June 8, 2015   119

TWENTY-TWO
What Is Reform? *The Strange Case of Greece and Europe*   122

TWENTY-THREE
What Can Happen in the Next Days?   127

TWENTY-FOUR
Bad Faith:
The IMF and Europe on Greece   130

TWENTY-FIVE
Only the "No" Can Save the Euro   134

TWENTY-SIX
Nine Myths About the Greek Referendum   138

Contents

TWENTY-SEVEN
What Is the Matter with Europe?   142

TWENTY-EIGHT
Exit Made Easy   145

TWENTY-NINE
Greece, Europe, and the United States   151

THIRTY
Plan B   155

THIRTY-ONE
Statement on the Ministry of Finance Working Group   159

THIRTY-TWO
A Note to the Editors at the *Guardian*   161

THIRTY-THREE
Death Spiral Ahead?   163

THIRTY-FOUR
The Future of Europe   168

THIRTY-FIVE
What the Greek Memorandum Means *with Daniel Munevar*   174

THIRTY-SIX
Back to Square Zero   181

Contents

THIRTY-SEVEN
A Final Word:
Madrid, October 21, 2015   185

Appendix: A Summary of Plan X   189
Acknowledgments   199
Notes   201

ONE

Welcome to the Poisoned Chalice

Welcome to the Poisoned Chalice

The modern Greek drama has its origins in the brutal German occupation of 1940–1944, in the British abandonment and betrayal of the Partisans that followed, in the ensuing civil wars, in the CIA-backed colonels' coup of 1967 and the dictatorship that followed, in the restoration of democracy in 1974, and in the introduction of a modern welfare state under Andreas Papandreou in the 1980s. It has origins in the turn to Europe engineered for Greece by Constantine Karamanlis and continued by Papandreou, in the ensuing corrupt waves of bank-financed military procurement and construction contracts, in the financial chicanery that covered Greece's ineligibility to join the Eurozone, and in the wave of borrowing, investment, construction, and debt-fueled growth that followed the introduction of the common currency in 1999. It was, from one point of view, an accident waiting to happen.

Yet if this were the whole story, it would be necessary to tell another one, equally good, for Spain, whose civil war came a decade earlier, for Ireland, whose civil war was a decade before that, and for Portugal, which never had a civil war. It would be necessary to explain why each of these countries fell into crisis at the same time and why others with equally fractured pasts and no stronger claim to business virtue—France, for instance, or Germany—did not. Most of all, these explanations would leave open a central question: Why did the crisis hit the peripheral countries of the euro and not so much those, such as Poland or Croatia, which had retained their national money?

In 1919, John Maynard Keynes wrote: "Europe is solid with herself. France, Germany, Italy, Austria and Holland, Russia and Roumania and Poland, throb together, and their structure and civilization are essentially one." This was of course untrue for the first seventy years after those words appeared, as Europe was rent by depression and autarky, and then by war and finally by the Iron Curtain, a division that most of us raised in the 1950s and 1960s, especially in America, were brought up not to expect to end. But it did end, in 1989, and then Germany reconstituted itself as the economic power at the core of Europe and the heart of the common currency, a hard money modeled on the gold standard and the Deutschemark.

There followed a remarkable development, perfectly understandable in retrospect but not widely foreseen when it mattered. Without a currency that could appreciate against those of her trading partners, German productivity increased and its technical excellence produced a declining real cost of exports, while in its European trading partners, deprived of currencies that could depreciate, stable purchasing power and easy credit produced a corresponding increase in demand for German goods. Meanwhile, Germany held down its internal wage levels while other countries allowed wages and unit labor costs to rise. The flow of goods from Germany to its markets was matched by a flow of credit, either directly to state purchasers of arms and infrastructure, as in Greece, or indirectly via private financing of residential and commercial construction booms, as in Spain and Ireland. In all cases the unbalanced flow of goods matched the accumulation of debts; the Greek instance was merely the most extreme. The Greek story is properly a European story in which, as in all European stories, Germany takes the leading role.[1]

If this helps us to see why Europe and the Eurozone plunged into crisis, it still does not explain why it all began to happen more or less at once, in 2010. The reason lies in the financial crisis of 2007–2009, which was a world crisis emanating from the United States. That crisis had its own origins, in a complex history of deregulation and desupervision going back four decades, culminating in the corruption and destruction of the vast US mortgage market under a series of presidents from Reagan through George W. Bush. Europeans became embroiled in this calamity in two ways: as the purchasers of US mortgage-backed securities and via parallel processes of internal deregulation and desupervision, in the context of historically close relations between banking elites and European states. So when the world financial crisis hit, it was no surprise that European banks would dump risk—in the form of peripheral country debts whether public or private—and turn to their national governments for help. Nor was it any surprise that the governments placed rescue of their own banks far above any concern for the consequences in Greece.[2] In this third way, the Greek drama is only an artifact, a side effect of the global banking and financial disaster.

From 2010 forward, these large forces intermingled and acted out on a small stage. The Hellenic Republic, a nation of islands and peninsulas on a distant edge of Europe, has just 3 percent of Europe's population and less than 2 percent of its gross output. It was (and still is) a stage of extreme effects. Greece had the largest deficits in precrisis Europe, well above 10 percent of GDP; it was forced to by far the greatest adjustment, moving to surplus within just a few years, mainly by cutting public spending, employment, and pensions, with more than 300,000 civil servants laid off. Greece accordingly suffered the largest economic and social collapse, losing more than 25 percent of its income; it labors still after five years under the largest external debts in relation to its GDP, and the highest rate of unemployment. The stress of daily life in Greece since 2010 has been enormous, and the country has been marked by rising rates of homelessness, emigration, and suicide—the social and psychological markers of economic failure.

My family engagement with Greece goes back seven decades. It is likely that my father first met Andreas Papandreou in the 1940s, and they were economist-colleagues at Harvard and Berkeley, respectively, in the 1950s. In April 1967, my father's intervention with Lyndon Johnson saved Andreas from execution at the hands of the colonels. (The message was relayed by phone at two o'clock in the morning: "Call Ken Galbraith, and tell him I've told those Greek bastards to lay off that son-of-a-bitch, whoever he is.")[3] My first return to Greece since childhood was not until 2006, to speak at an event honoring Andreas ten years after his death. In a cathedral-like setting, to a large and somber crowd of political and academic figures, including the entire Papandreou family, I read out that punch line.

When George Papandreou became prime minister in October 2009, I responded to an invitation to visit, advise, and (mostly) lend moral support. My role over several visits was insubstantial. Papandreou had run on a social welfare and economic growth platform that was swiftly overturned by the financial and debt crisis. By May 2010 he was forced to accept an austerity program as the price of a massive loan to avert the collapse of the Greek banking system, which was deeply invested in the unpayable debts of the Greek state. With that loan, power over economic policy passed to a committee of creditor institutions—the European Commission, the European Central Bank, and the International Monetary Fund—the infamous troika. Austerity, in turn, was supposed to make it more probable that the Greek state would be able to service its new and old debts.

At the time, Dominique Strauss-Kahn, a French Socialist, was managing director of the IMF and widely regarded as a progressive force as well as the future leader of a more progressive France. That soon-to-be-shattered illusion was only a small part of an entire pyramid of hopes and delusions—for a "New Deal," a "Green New Deal," a "Marshall Plan"—that progressives briefly entertained in the slipstream of the financial crisis. In reality, IMF staff and board members from Australia, China, Switzerland, and elsewhere already knew that the Greek debt was unsustainable and that Strauss-Kahn had ignored their reservations in order to push through, in 2010, what was at thirty-two times Greece's quota (or ownership share in the IMF) the largest IMF loan in relation to quota in history. The political reason was straightforward, though unspoken: the rescue was for the banks, not for Greece, and Strauss-Kahn wanted the French bankers' gratitude as he geared up his presidential bid.

A similar motive animated Jean-Claude Trichet, then president of the European Central Bank, another nominal Socialist and lifelong friend to the French bankers. In 2010, Trichet intervened by purchasing Greek bonds on the open market at a deep discount—thus supporting their price. The effect, since the bonds held by the ECB have to be serviced at face value, was to create an enduring debt burden for Greece that would otherwise have been reduced when, in 2012, Greece's debts were partly restructured. In this way, Europe and the IMF committed a financial fraud: extending a new loan to a bankrupt in order to defer inevitable losses. The notionally more conservative counterparts to these gentlemen in French government at the time, President Nicolas Sarkozy and his finance minister, Christine Lagarde, raised no objections. Nor did the German federal chancellor, Angela Merkel.

So the French and the German banks were saved, along with the Greek subsidiaries of the French banks, on whose books rested a good share of the Greek public debt. The unpayable Greek debts were assumed by the IMF, the ECB, and some new mechanisms for bilateral lending, the European Financial Stability Fund (EFSF) and later the European Stability Mechanism (ESM), which managed loans that in effect came from taxpayers throughout the Eurozone, including from those in some countries, such as Slovakia, that are less wealthy than Greece. What should have been a commercial write-down, requiring recapitalization of the French, German, and Greek banks, became instead a grand experiment in outside control: economic policy run by a creditors' cartel.[4]

To make the deal work, the IMF perjured itself on two points. First, it alleged that the Greek debt was "sustainable," a de facto precondition for Fund investment. Second, while it projected correctly that the inevitable sharp fiscal adjustment would produce a recession in 2011, it forecast that under the memorandum output would decline only by about 5 percent of GDP, with a full recovery by 2013. But staff and some board members had warned that things would be much worse,[5] and they were right: over the following years Greek output dropped 25 percentage points and did not recover. The collapse was about three times as severe as that in any other European state, about twice as bad as the worst recessions of the postwar period in any developed Western country, comparable to the Great Depression of the 1930s in the United States, and within hailing distance of the aftermath of the fall of the USSR.

In the spring of 2011, I became aware of a protean voice speaking with unique force and clarity on what was happening in his homeland. He was Yanis Varoufakis, a Greek with English economics training, Australian and Greek passports, and a Marxist-mathematical-philosophical academic background. A prolific blogger and critic of the austerity regime, Yanis was also the coauthor, with an old friend of mine, the former Labour MP Stuart Holland, of the *Modest Proposal*, a pamphlet setting out ideas for stabilizing Europe within the framework of the existing treaties.[6] It was detailed, ingenious, practical, and closely aligned with my own thinking. I wanted to meet him.

The chance came in October 2011, when I came to Athens to give a speech (and incidentally to see Papandreou in the last days of his tenure, just as the drama of the abandoned referendum[7] that led to his downfall was about to unfold), Yanis invited me to give a seminar in the Ph.D. program at the University of Athens. Shortly thereafter he came to Austin to keynote a conference I organized on the future of the Eurozone. Within a few months, thanks to the good work of the LBJ School dean, Robert Hutchings, he was recruited to Texas as a visiting professor, arriving in January 2013. There followed two years of close cooperation, including my co-authorship of the final version of the *Modest Proposal*, and a second Austin conference on the Eurozone, which featured a speech by the then-new leader of SYRIZA, the coalition of parties of the radical Left, a supposedly dangerous radical and political outsider named Alexis Tsipras.[8]

I first met Alexis in Athens in 2012, and again in June 2013 in Thessaloniki, the day the government shut down the Greek public radio and television service, ERT, supposedly for budget reasons, in effect depriving Greece of any television or radio not controlled by private oligarchs. The staff responded by occupying the buildings and continuing to broadcast over the Internet; Yanis and I went to the occupied ERT headquarters and met Tsipras there. Rebellion was brewing.[9]

On May 25, 2014, the night of the European Parliament elections, I was with Alexis and Yanis at SYRIZA headquarters when the party emerged as the largest in Greece. Two days later, following a private lunch with Alexis and one aide, Nikos Pappas (later minister of state), Yanis and I repaired to the studio of his wife, Danae Stratou, to draft a call on Chancellor Merkel to accept the election verdict and allow Jean-Claude Juncker to ascend to the presidency of the European Commission. This was not because Juncker was qualified for the job—as a lifelong functionary of a tax haven, he was not—but because otherwise the popular elections just conducted for that post would have been meaningless. SYRIZA released the statement, and within a few hours Merkel dropped her opposition. The link between these two events, if there was one, remains unknown.

That fall in Austin, Yanis and I watched as SYRIZA held its lead in the Greek polls, and we waited on the tense days in late December that, thanks to peculiarities of the Greek constitution, would decide whether Parliament would be dissolved and elections called. These had to do with the supermajority required to appoint a new president for the Hellenic Republic; as it turned out, there was no supermajority, elections were called for January 25, and Yanis returned to Athens, resigned his Texas post, and ran for Parliament. He was elected with the largest plurality in Greece. On January 26 he became finance minister, and I received an email, "Get here as soon as you can."

I arrived on February 8, by which time Yanis had completed his first (and famous) tour to Paris, London, and Berlin, making a splash in the papers by turning up at 11 Downing Street in a leather jacket.[10] It was the evening Parliament was to open with the prime minister's speech—the Greek equivalent of the queen's speech or the American state of the union. I made my way through the shabby entrance of the Ministry of Finance and up the rundown elevators to the sixth floor to the minister's office, a place of no glamour except for a full-on view of Parliament across Syntagma Square. In the minister's suite that evening there were, apart from two secretaries, no staff, no official computers, and no documents; Wi-Fi would start working the next day. Someone had left an icon on the shelf behind the ministerial desk; it would still be there five months later. My friend's first words to me were, "Welcome to the poisoned chalice."

That evening we walked together across the square to watch Alexis speak. Yanis had forsworn security—he would later accept plainclothes escorts—and dismissed the heavy German limos used by his predecessors, preferring to commute to work (and otherwise get around Athens) on his Yamaha. It was immediately clear that security was superfluous; the man had eleven million bodyguards. Drivers tooted or stopped to shake his hand; schoolgirls passing in a group broke ranks and swarmed; a city bus driver stopped, opened his window and saluted. Everywhere we were shadowed by people holding up cell phone video cameras. In the midst of the hubbub, Yanis asked, "Will they still be with us when the banks close?" On the way back from the prime minister's speech, after outrunning the press,[11] Yanis was accosted by a destitute middle-aged woman. He stopped to listen to her for five minutes or so, his hand on her arm; she was a cleaning lady, illegally fired and out of work for two years, seeking a job for her daughter. "What am I supposed to do with this?" Yanis asked, as he pocketed the daughter's resumé.

That first night, we worked until 2 A.M. before finally going out to eat. The only place open was a cafeteria perhaps half a mile away, a haunt for late dates and workers on the night shift. Everyone in the place came over to shake the new minister's hand. (At a taverna two nights later, the owner stopped by to tear up the bill.) Yanis had forgotten—so he said—how to eat; the second night I had to go out for breakfast, on my own, at 8:30 P.M. On the third night we were up until five in the morning, preparing documents for the first trip to Brussels. As we took our first (my only) motorcade ride with the prime minister's party out to his plane later that morning, there was a rare dusting of snow on the Athens hills.

My tasks for the Greek finance ministry were mostly incidental; Yanis Varoufakis is his own economist, his own politician, and his own speechwriter. I am not a technical person, and anyway the detailed business of the finance ministry, managing debt and collecting taxes, is done in Greek. I was there as a friend, unpaid and unofficial.[12] I could assist with policy documents, help handle or deflect the international press, maintain contact with parts of the US government, including the Treasury, the Federal Reserve, and (later) the White House. I could also write and speak about the situation as a close observer, as I did many times. Nothing I did or learned was confidential except in passing, as document drafts and position papers were composed and refined—until Yanis asked me to coordinate the "Plan B" exercise, the exit scenario from the euro, as a precaution in case negotiations failed. That effort had to remain entirely secret, and did so until Yanis chose to disclose it, following his resignation.[13]

During these months, I was not in Athens very much. In February, I was there for three days before emplaning with the government for a tense and dreary week in Brussels. In March, I sandwiched in another four days between speeches in Brussels and London and I did not return until the start of June. In April and May, I worked from Texas, Washington, and Paris, keeping close touch with colleagues in London, Zurich, Stockholm, Los Angeles, and New York—an exercise in virtuality. For the final month of the drama, from June 4 to July 7, I was in Greece (but partly on Crete) except for a week in Italy, in the comfortable care of my close friend the former Italian finance minister Giuseppe Guarino.

The broad chronology of events is the following. On January 25, the elections brought SYRIZA to power, in a political upheaval not seen in western Europe for perhaps five decades. The government formed immediately by coalition with a small right-wing party called AN-EL, the Independent Greeks, a xenophobic, homophobic fragment with which SYRIZA shared nothing except opposition to austerity; but since AN-EL was willing to overlook every one of its own positions in the interest of holding power, it was in its way the ideal coalition partner. Parliament opened on February 8; on the 12th the government flew to Brussels to start negotiations. These were urgent because the previous government, a coalition under Antonio Samaras between the conservative New Democracy and Papandreou's PASOK, had, along with the creditors, laid numerous traps for the incoming team, including payment deadlines and a February 28 termination date for the entire program of financial assistance.[14]

The Greek objective was to extend that deadline and to buy time to negotiate a new arrangement, while maintaining the financial support for the banking system necessary to prevent financial collapse. On February 20, after some hard wrangling, the Greeks achieved an interim agreement. They also had some immediate political requirements, especially to remove the intrusive, overbearing presence of troika bureaucrats in the Athens ministries. Eventually an awkward agreement was reached whereby the teams met technical staff in an Athens hotel, while policy discussions were confined to Brussels. The creditors hated the confinement, which made them invisible to the Greek public; but it was also not advantageous to the Greeks, who were obliged to station a team in Brussels for most of the five months. Eventually this team circumvented the Varoufakis ministry on key issues, and its leader, George Chouliarakis, became interim finance minister when new elections were called in August.

The issues to be negotiated fell into four main areas, each representing, at the beginning, a "red line" for the new government, meaning a question on which the government could not concede. The overarching macroeconomic question was "How much austerity?" and this was expressed as a target for the "primary surplus"— the excess of tax receipts over public spending without counting interest or principal payments on the national debt. With interest payments structured to be relatively low and indeed largely deferred until the 2020s, a large primary surplus would mean funds available to repay debt, and thereby lower the ratio of debt to GDP for Greece, eventually, it was said, with the effect of restoring direct access to the private bond markets. For this reason, the creditors wanted a primary surplus target of 4.5 percent of GDP, to be reached through large increases in the value-added tax (VAT) as well as spending cuts. The difficulty was that any such attempt was self-defeating: the more you raise taxes and cut spending in a depressed economy, the smaller your GDP and the higher your debt-to-GDP ratio. Greece had been on that treadmill for years, and since 2009 the ratio had gone from about 100 percent to 170 percent even though its debt had not risen by nearly 70 percent. The country was bankrupt, and there was no realistic scenario under which the debt, even after it was restructured in 2012, could be repaid. The creditors knew these facts, but they were disposed to ignore them. As one observer put it, "The institutions don't do macroeconomics."

Pensions were a second sensitive question. The Greek population is relatively elderly, and the country lacks an effective system of unemployment insurance. In the crisis, many people who were thrown out of work took early retirement, and pension costs jumped. At the same time, unemployment and increasing amounts of off-the-books labor (estimated at 30 percent by 2015) meant that contributions to the pension system were down, and the pension funds were cut roughly in half when Greek public debt was haircut in 2012. The result was that pension costs as a share of GDP were very high—about 16 percent—even though pension benefits had been cut between 44 and 49 percent and the median Greek pension, around 650 euros a month, was barely above the poverty line. Many pensioners were receiving just 350 euros. The creditors demanded further cuts, and the government resisted.

A third key issue concerned Greek labor markets. Here the creditors had insisted on cutting minimum wages and on dismantling the Greek system of trade union organization and collective bargaining, effectively disenfranchising one of Europe's most militant working classes. The ostensible economic objective was "internal devaluation" to "restore competitiveness," and this brought two problems. First, cutting wages and incomes without providing any relief from private debts (such as fixed mortgages) merely deepens debt burdens and forces people into bankruptcy and foreclosure. This is the problem of "debt deflation," which had become severe in Greece by 2014, when both prices and nominal incomes were falling. Second, when wages fell, Greek businesses did not cut prices proportionately; instead they raised profit margins, pocketing the difference and (surely in many cases) moving it out of the country. Thus exports and competitiveness did not recover; an "improved" trade balance came about through a sharp reduction in consumption and therefore imports.

The fourth area was privatization. SYRIZA was philosophically opposed—or at least deeply skeptical—of privatization as an economic strategy, but the new government did not choose to fight the issue on ideological grounds. Instead it argued for pragmatic alternatives: that the Greek government should retain an equity stake in most privatizations, that it should pace the process so as to receive decent prices, and that it should avoid simply transforming public utilities, such as electricity and water, into private monopolies. In the case of the Port of Piraeus, in line for sale to the state-owned Chinese firm Cosco, one had the interesting postmodern twist of a left-wing government in a capitalist country imposing labor standards on a right-wing company from a communist country.

There were many other issues under negotiation, including the organization and control of Greek statistical services and the tax authority, civil service issues (including the government's decision to rehire two thousand cleaning ladies illegally dismissed under Samaras), and the structure of VAT rates on hotels and restaurants and in the Greek islands. It is habitual in Europe for islands to benefit from lower VAT rates, but the creditors did not agree to this for Greece. There were also such narrow questions as the expiration date on milk (in Greece shelf life had been three days, the creditors wanted seven so as to extend market access to Dutch dairies), and whether pharmacies could be taken over by chains. The relation of most of these issues to Greek "competitiveness" was remote—they reflect the lobbying of northern European companies—but this did not stop the creditors from sugarcoating their demands with the fine language of "structural reform."

Then there was an issue that never made it to the negotiating table: the size and structure of the Greek external public debt. Here, in a nutshell, the problem was that the IMF requires a "debt sustainability analysis" showing an ongoing decline in the debt-to-GDP ratio before it can sign on to a financial program.[15] As the IMF had traduced this requirement in 2010, staff and non-European board members were properly determined not to let it happen again. So even though Greek interest payments had been reduced and much principal deferred in 2012, the IMF agreed with Greece that further restructuring remained essential. The European creditors, and especially Germany and the ECB, would have none of it. For them, to restructure the Greek debt again would mean confessing the original sin: their failure to write it down when the crisis started.

So negotiations began. But as March turned to April, it became ever more apparent to the Greek team that in fact there were no negotiations. The Greek side would prepare a position, usually making some concession as a show of good faith, and present it to the institutions in Brussels. The answer would come back quickly: *not good enough.* There would be no counterproposal. Creditors would leak complaints to the press that the Greeks had no positions, that they were wasting time, posturing, gambling.[16] The lazy punditry adverted many times to Yanis's interest in the economic theory of games, ignoring the fact that as an academic economist he was a critic, not an advocate, of game theory. The German press and the Greek private media went over to a campaign of character assassination.[17] The British newspapers, notably the *Guardian* and the *Financial Times,* relayed the Brussels spin to the Anglo-American world. Defense came only from a few columnists, including the excellent Ambrose Evans-Pritchard at the euroskeptic *Telegraph,* Wolfgang Munchau at the *Financial Times,* and Larry Elliott in the *Guardian.*

On March 23 at Riga, the European finance ministers lowered the boom on Yanis, leaking a false story to the effect that he had been roundly denounced by all of his counterparts at the meeting. Since Eurogroup meetings are held in private, with no official transcript, it was extremely difficult to counter this message, and from this point his position inside the Greek government began to slip.[18] There emerged in the prime minister's circles a "troika of the interior" who held the view that Greece would have to accept whatever deal was ultimately offered. Negotiations should therefore proceed on the basis of ongoing concessions, beginning with accepting the principle of a large primary surplus—3.5 percent, hardly better than the 4.5 percent demanded by the creditors. This concession, essentially conceived in political terms by the prime minister's circle, cemented the case for tax increases and spending cuts while undercutting the argument for debt reduction.

Further concessions would follow, but nothing worked. The creditors had only one bottom line, which was a return to the memorandum of understanding as signed in 2014, with no material changes. Their point of leverage would come at the moment the Greek state ran out of money.

From the start of the process, the European Central Bank held Greece's fate in its hands. Greek banks had funded themselves by discounting Greek government bonds directly with the ECB, under a waiver provided to cover for the fact that the debt was not investment grade. On February 4, 2015, the ECB revoked the waiver, forcing the Greek banks to rely on another channel, emergency liquidity assistance, which the ECB ran through the Bank of Greece. This facility was subject to a ceiling, and the ECB proceeded by raising that ceiling in small stages, every week or so, so that Greek bank depositors were constantly reminded that the security of their money hung by a thread. Meanwhile non-Greek banks withdrew lines of credit, forcing the Greek banks to rely ever more heavily on the ECB. Depositors and bankers alike were well aware of this, and from December onward a fear campaign associated with the election deepened people's anxieties. By the time the Tsipras government took office, new financial activity had virtually stopped.

The Greek state, meanwhile, faced a series of debt repayments, which ordinarily would have been refinanced. But this too the creditors now refused. And so Greece was forced to drain its reserves, requisition funds from towns, universities, and hospitals, and default to suppliers in order to meet the lump-sum cash demands of the institutions. This Greece did, to the tune of 3.5 billion euros, until early June, when the last funds ran out. At that point, a scheduled payment to the IMF had to be delayed, by a little-used device of "bundling" it with other payments due that month, and putting it all back to the end of June. At that point the pressures converged: the squeeze on the banks, the squeeze on the government, and the expiration date of the extended program. All of this placed the negotiating team, then led by Euclid Tsakalotos, under intense pressure.[19] The question came down to the red lines—the primary surplus, labor markets, pensions, and privatizations—which Alexis Tsipras had spelled out very clearly from the beginning. The question was: Could he be forced to step across those lines?

It was in full anticipation of this moment that Yanis Varoufakis asked me, back in late March, to begin preparation for Plan B—or Plan X as we called it—an outline of what would have to be done if negotiations failed and Greece were forced to exit the euro. This I did, over about six weeks, relying on financial and legal help and a very small amount of local expertise. It was in many ways an academic exercise, of reading and summarizing and rethinking other people's published work, as academics do.

The political sensitivity of the question required absolute secrecy, which limited both our communications and what we could learn. Our prognosis for a hostile exit was never optimistic, and as we listed issues and challenges it became less so—to a degree that, I now believe, overstated the difficulties and overlooked some promising ways around them. In the end it did not matter; although there was (I later learned) one high-level meeting on the issue, the prime minister did not seek a briefing from us, and work on the question ended for practical purposes with the submission of a long memorandum in early May.

In the end, Greece's fate hinged on the politics of Europe, and in no way on the technical questions of economics or tactics of negotiation. The politics were highly adverse. The east Europeans and the Finns have right-wing governments wholly opposed to the Greek Left, and in the Baltics and Slovakia the tension is aggravated by the fact that the Greeks are wealthier than they are. The Spaniards, Portuguese, and Irish had rising Left oppositions of their own—Podemos, the Left Bloc, Sinn Fein—and opposed any concessions that might fuel those flames. The Germans and the institutions had both ideology and power to defend. In no sense were the finance ministers assembled in the Eurogroup or the midlevel technocrats delegated by the EC, ECB, and IMF either disposed or empowered or intellectually suited to take on board the Greek arguments. To such people, argument is pro forma—what matters is who pays the bills, and who holds the votes.

For this reason the Greek strategy became one of getting a decision at the "political level"—the level of great power politics, of the US-Russia conflict over Ukraine. In Europe, that meant turning the resolution of the crisis into a test of German leadership. It was, therefore, on the unlikely person of Chancellor Angela Merkel that Greek diplomacy had to fasten its only hope.

The route to Merkel was in part direct, in part through Paris and Rome, in part through Washington, and it is fair to say that friends of Greece made heroic efforts on all these fronts, not entirely without results.[20] President Obama several times picked up the phone and made sympathetic calls, although in other respects the US government had little leverage and did not use what it had.[21] In the end Merkel was not to be turned; for her the possibility of simply crushing Tsipras, Varoufakis, and SYRIZA was always a live option, and in the tumult of the referendum called on June 28 as the negotiations collapsed, that was the path she chose. It would not, after all, be the first time she had swatted down a Left government in Greece, and SYRIZA had held out for a good deal longer than PASOK.

I returned to Greece from a week in Italy on July 3, into the tumult of the referendum campaign. At the finance ministry I found Yanis glum, frustrated that the government had not waged a vigorous No campaign, a bit awed by the campaign of fear and intimidation—terrorism, he called it—being mounted on Greek television, and resigned to a victory of the Yes. I did not think so, and the twin rallies that evening reinforced my view. At the No rally, the largest in the history of the Greek Republic, Yanis was mobbed on arrival. I merely took the subway, emerging in the middle of the crowd, and stood alongside the stolid, determined, largely unemotional assembly. Within a few minutes, two older men sidled up to me and extended their hands. "Thank you for what you are doing for Greece."

The writings that follow tell their own story of these years and months, which led to the magnificent 61.5 percent No of July 5, to Yanis's resignation on July 6, and thence to the government's capitulation to its creditors' demands on July 13, to the new memorandum, to the split within SYRIZA, and finally to the resignation of Alexis Tsipras and new elections, which reformed the original coalition between SYRIZA and AN-EL. What will happen politically in Greece over the next few years is anyone's guess. But for the moment the economic die is cast, the policies are locked in, and their outcomes will unfold over time. It would take a new and even sterner revolution to block the process, and for the moment, the prospect of that is dim.

So what will happen? In economic matters one is never entirely sure; Greece is a small country and the deus ex machina of foreign investment, a tourist boom, a military crisis, or something else could always supervene. But on the most likely course, they won't. And so the Greek state, Greek businesses, and households will continue on their downward trend, with tax shortfalls leading to spending cuts, loan defaults to foreclosures, and bankruptcies leading ultimately to a foreign takeover of the banking system. Meanwhile the country will be transformed, its marketable assets and real estate sold out. Greece will become something much less like a proud and self-sufficient European nation, and much more like (say) a Caribbean dependency of the United States. Its professional population will continue to leave, and its working classes will also either emigrate or sink into destitution. Or perhaps they will fight.

In a world where so many countries have suffered this treatment—where outside certain charmed circles it is practically routine—does it matter if one more small and distant place is added to the list? Perhaps not. But Greece is a bit closer to our sensibilities than other places. Its familiarity, its link to the concept of democracy, its European identity are, for better or worse, distinctive. The place pulls at us, it evokes the words that Keynes applied to Germany in 1919:

> The policy . . . of degrading the lives of millions of human beings, and of depriving a whole nation of happiness should be abhorrent and detestable—abhorrent and detestable, even if it were possible, even if it enriched ourselves, even if it did not sow decay of the whole civilized life of Europe.

But I would add two more reasons, also weighty and honorable. The first is that in the person of Yanis Varoufakis the Greeks had for five months a spokesman of merit, who could and did articulate their case and call it to the attention of the world. That's rare. The second is that when they were given the chance, the Greek people stood up. They said "No" and they were prepared, at that moment, to pay the price.

This places an obligation—a moral obligation—on all of us to stand with them.

The essays that follow are presented substantially as they were written at the time. I have added footnotes here and there, to clarify certain points or to explain references that may be obscure. I make no claim that every judgment in these pages was borne out; only that the stream of narrative will give the reader a fair impression of how the Greek drama unfolded, as seen from my vantage point.

TOWNSHEND, VERMONT
September 1, 2015

PART I

2010–2014

TWO

Europe's Crisis

Thinking It Through to the End

In early January, the Greek government convened an emergency meeting of expert advisers.[1] A man from the IMF told the prime minister flatly that the only way out was to dismantle the welfare state. A man from the OECD[2] jovially proposed a test: when all your supporters are fighting mad, he said, you'll know you've done enough.

The theory behind these arguments held that bond buyers judge the determination of the government's austerity programs and then decide whether to trust in the repayment of debt. Given sufficiently harsh and credible measures, interest rates would fall and the refinancing could proceed.

But there was a problem: for the policy to work, the cuts have to be carried out. Implementation takes time. Refinancing depends on confidence in the austerity package, before the cuts are actually made. And how can a mere policy announcement engender such belief? Whatever was said, when Greece's current bonds matured,

Le Monde Diplomatique, May 2010

the actual cuts would still lie ahead. And the fact was, the more severe the announced program, the less credible it would be.

This argument logically destroyed the notion that *any* austerity
program would reopen private bond markets on acceptable terms.
The only way to avoid default was for Europe to refinance the
Greek debt, and the question became: how to persuade Europe to
do so?

Thus austerity became a political game. The Greek government
still had to announce severe cuts—not to pacify the markets but to
meet the needs of Angela Merkel. Her voters would not tolerate a
"bailout" unless they saw painful sacrifices from the Greeks. Meanwhile the Greek government declared unshakable allegiance to its
debt and to the euro—while subtly reminding Paris and Berlin that
default and exit could not be excluded if help did not come.

This game made no economic sense for Europe. Greek deflation
would mean joblessness, lost tax revenues, and therefore little actual deficit reduction in Greece. You cannot cut 10 percent of GDP
from total demand without cutting GDP itself. Falling Greek GDP
would cost jobs for German and French factory workers. Greece's
ability to service its debts would not improve. Nor—absent a devaluation, made impossible by the euro—would the country's competitiveness get better. The measures that might help over time,
namely the program of public administration and tax reforms to
which the Greek government was already committed—would be
much harder to implement in the atmosphere of crisis, cuts, and
high interest rates.

As the debt deadline neared, Europe's leaders labored under ar-
cane rules, an unwieldy collective process, domestic political back-
lash, and the burden of their own limited understanding. Predict-
ably, they came to the verge of disaster. After Chancellor Merkel
appeared to repudiate a funding package, panic swept the Eurozone, and the price of credit default swaps on Portugal, Spain, and

their banks soared. Merkel blinked, and a re-funding package went through, with a contribution from the IMF.[3]

But now came a second epiphany. The Greek bond bailout only made the European financial crisis worse. To see why, imagine you own a Portuguese bond. Repayment is uncertain, so you dump it, or purchase a credit default swap. The bond price then falls, making Portugal's refinancing harder. In the limit, the best way to assure payment is to *close* the private bond markets and blackmail the European Union to come in with a "rescue package." Which cannot be denied, for everyone understands that Portugal has not been so "irresponsible" as Greece. The game of chicken escalates. And after Portugal, there is Spain.

The speculators could thus force the Europeanization of Mediterranean debts, and in mid-May this happened with breathtaking speed. There was panic—just as in the United States in September 2008—and for the same reason. Like all victims of blackmail, President Sarkozy expressed anger, warning darkly of the wrath of the EU. But what can it do? A bond sale or credit default swap on Greece, Portugal, or Spain can be consummated entirely outside Europe—say in New York or the Cayman Islands. And when the finance ministers announced their joint defense of eurobonds, the speculators only regrouped for another attack.

The huge scale of the EU defense calmed things for a moment. But it will become clear, soon enough, that the EU governments can only borrow from each other. They cannot create net new reserves and they cannot finance growth and bond bailouts at the same time. Only the European Central Bank can do that, and at first reports the actual role of the ECB remained vague.

And so a third pillar of financial wisdom begins to come clear. In a successful financial system, there must be a state larger than any market. That state must have monetary control—as the Federal Reserve does, without question, in the United States. Otherwise, the markets play divide and conquer against the states. Europe has devoted enormous effort to create a "single market" without enlarging any state, and while pretending that the Central Bank cannot provide new money to the system. In so doing, it has created markets larger than states, and states with unbearable debts, which now consume them.

So while the EU rearranges the deck chairs, the ship founders. Each country gets, in turn, just enough assistance to repay its debts. The price, each time, is massive budget cuts. The banks are saved, but growth, jobs, and the achievements of the welfare state are destroyed. The IMF man gets his way. And the European recession grows deeper and deeper.

The European crisis will therefore continue, until Europe changes its mind. It will continue until the forces that built the welfare state in the first place rise up to defend it. It will continue until Europe faces the *constitutional* deficiencies of its system. Europe needs a single integrated tax structure, the routine recycling of funds from surplus to deficit regions, a central bank dedicated to economic prosperity, and a cutting-down of the financial sector.

The cutdown can be achieved in three ways: by regulation, by taxation, and by restructuring the debts of the Mediterranean states. For this, Europe needs a sovereign insolvency process comparable to Chapter IX covering municipal bankruptcy in US law—as long proposed from Vienna by Professor Kunibert Raffer.[4] That would permit national governments to maintain essential services while relieving themselves of unpayable debts.

The end result will be a European superstate, capable of supporting public expenditure at a fiat interest rate, without regard to the ratings agencies or the CDS markets. It will be a state in firm control of its banks—and not controlled by them. The model for such a state exists. It is the United States, a nation whose fundamental economic structure was built, decades ago, in a similar crisis by Franklin Roosevelt in the New Deal.[5]

At that point, a fourth pillar of wisdom will come into view: that the goal of economic policy cannot be to satisfy the gods of the bond market. It is to provide economic opportunity—full employment, education, health care, and decent pensions—to the people. And to solve, so far as possible, the larger environmental and energy problems that we all face.

Pray for wisdom to come soon. For if not, the pain will continue for years and years.

THREE

Greece and the European Project

The collapse of the Soviet empire in 1989 and of the USSR in 1991 have become walled off in Western minds as events from an alien time and place. But they should remind us that the architecture of human governments is not eternal. Communism was once a powerful threat to its capitalist rivals. But when circumstances change, the bright hopes of an age are prone to crash in disillusion.

Europe was a bright political project at the formation of the European Community and again when it expanded at the end of the Cold War. Its purpose was not so much power as peace: truly a noble vision. But that noble project was built on an end-of-history economics, on frozen-in-time free-market notions, and on dogmatic monetarism linked to arbitrary criteria for deficits and public debt. In the wake of a global financial meltdown, these no longer serve. Unless they are abandoned soon, they will doom Europe as surely as communism doomed the empire of the East.

Deutsche Welle, July 2011

Europe's structure is also suspended between two stable formations: the federated nation-state and the international alliance. This in-between structure is called a *confederacy*, and it is something that was tried and which failed in North America on two occasions, most recently in 1865. The South lost the US Civil War, in part, because it left too much power in the hands of the individual states, and so could not in the end raise the funds or the men required to keep its armies in the field. And following defeat, it took almost seventy years—until Roosevelt's New Deal in 1933—before sufficient measures were taken to begin to overcome the dire poverty and economic stagnation of that region. This history, too, has been walled off in modern minds.

The distinctive combination of millenarian economic ideas and unstable political structure faced a powerful shock from the global meltdown. Faced with vast holdings of toxic US assets, investors sought to cut their losses by selling weak and small sovereigns: Greece, Ireland, Portugal, Spain. Thus yields soared on those debts, while they fell simultaneously on US, German, French, and British bonds. There was no sudden discovery that Greece was ill-managed or that Ireland had had an unsustainable construction boom. Those facts were known. The new event was the meltdown, the flight to safety, and the waves of predatory speculation that have followed.

Therefore what happened was a solvency crisis of the banks, as always happens in debt crises. It was true in the 1980s, when the Reagan administration, no less, felt obliged to prepare a secret plan to nationalize all the major New York banks should a single major Latin American debtor declare default.[1] It was true in 2008–2009, when preventing the imminent collapse of Bank of America, Citigroup, and the others trumped all other US policy concerns. It is obvious that the entire recent thrust of European policy has been to find ways to paper over the problems of Europe's banks: with phony stress tests, with new loans, with loud talk, with denunciations of profligacy in Greece or anywhere else—with anything except an honest examination of what lies at the heart of the problem.

Today Greece—under a resolute government and against heavy internal protest—has met the onerous conditions imposed on it. But for what? For loans that are immediately recycled to Europe, adding nothing to Greece's prospects except more debt? This will not lower interest rates, restore growth, or bring success to ongoing internal reforms. It is an intolerable situation, and it will not continue for long.

Along one road there lies a future of defaults, panic, dissolution of the Eurozone, and hyperinflation in the exiting countries, with a collapse of the export markets for those that remain. The final consequence will be large population movements—as happened from the American South. For if Europe insists on reducing its periphery to poverty, it cannot expect those affected to sit still and accept their fate.[2]

Along the other road lies the assumption of common responsibilities for sustained convergence, based on a new economics of mutual support. Along this path sovereign debts below the Maastricht ceiling will be taken over and converted to European bonds and there will be a public-private investment program to restore growth and employment—as some of Europe's wisest leaders demanded in a manifesto just a few days ago.[3] There will follow in due course the constitutional reforms needed to adapt Europe and its policies to the conditions of the postcrisis world.

Europe must therefore choose, and soon, as de Gaulle said in 1969, "*entre le progrès et le bouleversement*"—between progress and upheaval.

FOUR

A Question of Moral Responsibility

Athens is a city on the edge, and not just because of the protests. It was the empty storefronts, the sleeping addicts, the beggars, and the squeegee men that caught my eye. And there was the polite conversation with working professionals about their 40 percent pay cuts and their escalating taxes, and about moving their money out of the country while they can. The data show total output falling at a 5 percent annual rate, but specialists are sure the final figures will be worse. The business leaders I spoke with all said there is no hope at all.

Greece is a country with weak institutions, and they are being destroyed. The schools and the hospitals and the university were never first-rate; now they are getting worse. It is a country with fairly low wages, and they are being driven down. It is a country

October 2011; published in 2012 by the Foundation for European Progressive Studies, in a pamphlet entitled "Austerity Is Not the Solution: Contributions to European Economic Policy," 19–23.

that had improved its infrastructure, thanks to easy credit and EU assistance and no doubt the good work of German engineering firms—but the improvements cannot be maintained. Greece has never been a very attractive spot for foreign investment, and it is becoming less so. Unemployment has always been high for young people; now there are practically no jobs at all.

It is obvious that nothing happening today in Greece will produce economic recovery or forestall default on the debt. On the contrary. Even though the Greek government refuses to take the step of defaulting, it will be forced into that position whenever the Germans and French pull the plug on new loans. This they are plainly preparing to do. Meanwhile, they are punishing the Greeks—in order to make sure that when Greece is permitted to default and restructure, the other peripheral countries and especially Italy will not be tempted down the same path.[1] This is called "ring-fencing." It is also called the principle of collective guilt, destroying the livelihoods of thirteen million people for political reasons.[2]

It is true that the Greek government was always a weak borrower. It is true that the country has a large civil service, a patronage-based politics, aggressive unions, and dubious accounts. Anyone who has worked there will tell you this. It is also true that this was no secret during the boom years. The lenders knew. Just as they knew that in Ireland commercial development was out of control, that in Spain it was housing, and that in the United States it was liar's loans to borrowers who could never pay. This is the way credit works. In the boom standards fall and in the slump they are stiffened, while the lenders pompously proclaim that "no one could have known."

The Greek government has accepted the terms imposed upon it, admitting more than its share in responsibility, especially given that this government was not in power during the boom years. It has cut, cut, and cut again. But the cuts and tax increases are never enough, and the "troika" comes back time and again for new measures, such as breaking the national wage bargain or (as I heard) using up funds held in reserve to protect the banks. (One has to ask: Who would not move their money out, under such conditions?) Looming in the background is a plan to place nearly all of Greece's public assets under private management from abroad—asset-stripping, in plain words. Though floated by a consultant, this was described to me, by a high European official, as the "secret German plan."[3]

This is economic policy as moral abomination. It is not designed to succeed as economics. It is failing because it is designed to fail. Europe's leaders know what they are doing. The policy is not intended to restore growth and prosperity; a policy whose clear effect over years and years is decline and destruction must have been actually intended to achieve that effect. So one must infer that when M. Barroso and M. Trichet and now M. Draghi prate on about "restoring the confidence of the markets," this is for the edification of children and dolts.[4] The only other possibility is that these leaders are incompetent beyond all reasonable imagining.

The purpose of punishment is twofold. First, it is to meet political needs in Germany and France, reaffirming the righteous self-sense in the upper-crust of those countries, who cannot accept that the lender is anything other than the offended party, the violated paragon of virtue and hard work. This parallels standard historical mythology for France, but Germans should know better, what with having been saddled at the Treaty of Versailles with sole responsibility for the First World War, and then the consequences of that. Keynes quoting Hardy comes to mind:

> Nought remains
> But vindictiveness here amid the strong,
> And there amid the weak an impotent rage.[5]

The second purpose is to preserve the French and German banks from the failure that will ensue when losses on all their bad loans have to be recognized. The banks can withstand a Greek write-down, more so in Germany than in France, which is why the German government is more open to this outcome than the French. But they cannot withstand a cascading series of defaults in the other peripheral countries, at least not all at once or in short order.

That cascade will come, sooner or later, as the debt burdens on Ireland, Portugal, Spain, Italy, and ultimately Belgium and France mount. Once Greece defaults, that Rubicon will be crossed, and it will be only a matter of time. Time, however, is important. What the policy may achieve is to string out the destruction, as it proceeds eventually from Greece to Ireland and on to other countries. The game is to destroy only one country at a time, keeping up the austerity programs and the debt payments in all the others for as long as possible, so that the effect of the popular rebellion now getting under way does not shake the foundations of the Eurozone.

But then again, maybe it won't even do that. Keynes again:

> If the European Civil War is to end with France and Italy abusing their momentary victorious power to destroy Germany and Austria-Hungary now prostrate, they invite their own destruction also, being so deeply and inextricably intertwined with their victims by hidden psychic and economic bonds.

There are technical solutions. The proposals, which have been worked over by men and women of earnest good will in all the European countries, involve European bonds, bank recapitalization, and an investment program. The solutions can work, and in their minimalist forms they are within the current framework of European law. They do require recognizing that the previous economic ideology of the European Union must be abandoned, and that the financial sector must bear losses that will require it to be restructured in whole or part.

But the obstacles are political, insofar as important constituencies in Germany and France oppose these measures, alongside outspoken fellow-travelers in Finland, Slovakia, and elsewhere. And they are financial, insofar as they would require recognition of losses to European banks that the banks and other parties continue to believe they can deny.

The issue therefore is whether the political leadership in Berlin and Paris is interested in technical solutions. It is plain enough that they are not. It is plain enough that Europe's leaders place their own political survival in first place, the survival of their banks second, that of the European project third, and the people of the periphery dead last. That being so, it is only a matter of time before desperate populations erupt in revolt, forcing a change of course— or a crack-up.

And the moral question in that case will come down to: which side are you on?

FIVE

Neither Austerity nor Growth

Solidarity Is Europe's Only Hope

The austerity moment is passing. Britain's double-dip recession and Europe's 11 percent unemployment show where austerity leads. Protests in Greece and Spain show the suffering it causes. Politics, so far in France, shows that voters will not tolerate it for long. At a recent conference in Berlin, high European Central Bank officials could cite only Latvia to support their claim that austerity works.[1] It was pathetic.

Now fashionable opinion offers the *growth* alternative. Growth means higher profits, better wages, and more jobs. What a fine idea. The problem is that growth is only a *goal*. It is not a *policy*. And every lobbyist, political hack, and ten-cent crank has a strategy to make growth happen.

The American rich urge tax cuts as a "growth strategy." In Europe, employers urge "labor market reform," just as bankers favor deregulation. And today both "stimulus" and "fiscal consolidation"

Le Monde, June 2012

are "pro-growth," depending on who you ask. Some adept thinkers favor both, one earlier and the other later; in this way they embrace cuts in pensions and health care as part of a "strategy for growth."

In truth, the protesters of Greece and Spain and Italy, the voters of France, and sympathizers of the Occupy Movement in America do not clamor for growth. What they most want is to protect the institutions and essentials that make their lives tolerable, safe, and attractive. These are health care, education, local public services, culture, the environment, and the right to retire in modest comfort at a reasonable age.

These citizens know where their interests lie. In modern life, schools, universities, clinics, hospitals, clean and safe streets, and a secure future are not expendable. They have become the central features of life, the sum and substance of desire and happiness. Cars, computers, liquor, and tobacco: these are the extras now. The companies who make them seek profits, and therefore growth. But the people would have solidarity instead, if they could.

In Europe's past, solidarity and social progress arose from war. In the United States it rose from slavery and the struggle for civil rights. Even in the New Deal blacks were at first excluded: mostly black farm workers were not covered by Social Security, and domestics were exempted from the minimum wage. Now the fight is mainly over the place of immigrants. Barriers remain, but the American moral tendency has been to reduce them, slowly, over time.

In Europe, the idea that solidarity must extend *across* nations has not yet taken hold. Germans never promised to pay Spanish pensions; they took it as a European principle that they would never have to. But today Spain is in debt trouble, and the issue is whether Spaniards can have any social protections—if they stay in Europe. The "European principle" thus threatens Europe itself.

For many Spaniards, Greeks, Portuguese, and Italians, preserving basic social protections is the most important thing. All of these countries have been *both* fascist and poor. Many of their citizens remember that fascism was worse.[2] Many supported joining Europe to build social democracy and bury the past. They object now to retrogression imposed from Brussels. And who can blame them?

In France today, President Hollande has rightly rejected the deceit of austerity. He should likewise keep his distance from the chimera of growth. The false slogans, half-measures, technical fixes, and appeals to prudence and confidence are rapidly falling before the panic mounting everywhere, right now.

The one hope is to embark on a new path of solidarity—protecting health, education, jobs, and retirement *throughout Europe*. But of course it's not really a new path. The great postwar gains of social democracy in France and Germany were exactly the same. And they were adopted because otherwise the stressed and damaged nations who needed them might have dissolved.

Now Europe must reaffirm these values for all Europeans—or Europe faces the same danger.

SIX

The Victory of SYRIZA Is Not Against American Interests

WITH YANIS VAROUFAKIS

The sudden closing of state television and radio on Tuesday night has sparked political drama in Greece.[1] ERT's journalists and staff occupied the buildings, the electric power union refused orders to turn off the lights, large crowds gathered to show support. With transmitters dark, broadcasting resumed over the Web, and soon radio and TV all over Europe were picking up the feeds. Overnight an organization reviled for corruption and cronyism became the voice of a democratic resistance.

We traveled to Thessaloniki on Wednesday in part to be interviewed at ERT3, the only branch of the state media that had not blacklisted Varoufakis since 2011. That interview did not happen. But at the ERT3 offices we met Alexis Tsipras, head of SYRIZA, the official Greek opposition, greeted the occupiers, and then walked to a nearby hall for an economic discussion that had acquired, suddenly, an audience of more than two thousand people. Next night

New York Times, June 2013

in Athens we got our interview, at two in the morning in the main ERT studios, now operating as a cooperative.

Why did Samaras close ERT?[2] Doing so met European demands for reduction in public workforce and for spending cuts, at a moment when negotiations to sell the gas monopoly to Gazprom had just failed. It squeezed the minor coalition partners, including the former ruling Socialist Party, which are now damned if they acquiesce and damned if they don't. If the partners don't fall in line, there will be new elections in which they will be destroyed, while Samaras's own chances are better now than they will be later, as economic conditions get worse. And—not least—closing ERT took all noncommercial political discourse and local news in Greece off the air.

But Samaras may have overreached. Despite its flaws, ERT is the only mass forum for public discourse that Greeks have. In closing it the government has turned a murky debate over austerity, confidence, and credit markets into an open fight over democracy and national independence. In that fight, SYRIZA—the party of the "radical left"—now stands as the alternative. Alexis Tsipras may therefore soon enough be prime minister of Greece.

What would a Tsipras government mean for the United States? In security terms, nothing vital would change. SYRIZA does not propose to leave NATO or to close US bases, for instance on Crete. It would be a bit much to say that US complicity in the dictatorship of 1967 to 1974 has been forgotten. And any Greek government will differ with the United States, to a degree, over the Middle East. But the fact is, Greece's problem today is with Europe, and Tsipras does not want to pick any fight with the United States.

The financial sector will view a SYRIZA victory with horror. But banks and hedge funds know that most Greek debt is held by the European official sector and the small remainder is being snapped up by investors because they know it will be paid. Big Finance is worried about the knock-on effects—about what may happen elsewhere if a democratic left party wins anywhere in Europe. This instinct is natural enough in bankers, even when they know that things must change. For the US government to adopt it would be strategically stupid.

For right now SYRIZA may be Europe's best hope. Greeks know that a breakup of the Eurozone will be harsh on them, that it would lead to the collapse of the zone as a whole and even of the European Union. They also know that the European approach to the crisis has failed. Therefore a collapse is coming, if ideas and policies do not change. Tsipras and SYRIZA represent this view. A new government in Greece will press for the reform and salvation of the European project.

The basic requirements for reform can be met within existing European treaties. They are a mutualization of debt service, restructuring of the European banks, an investment and jobs program, and a European initiative to meet the social and human crisis by strengthening unemployment insurance, basic pensions, deposit insurance, and core public institutions like education and health. In Greece, hunger is rising in and out of the schools. SYRIZA plans to fight hunger and the Nazi party, Golden Dawn, with school lunches and food stamps.[3]

A campaign to change ideas must start somewhere. With the events this week at ERT, it may have started here in Greece, a small, proud country that has, in the past, given quite a few ideas to the world. Including one, people's government, that we like to call by its Greek name.

SEVEN

The United States and Europe

What Is Going On?

The recent growth news has been good in America and bad in Europe, which—as it should—prompts the question, why?

Fifteen years ago there would have been an immediate confident mainstream answer. The United States was then celebrated for its flexible labor markets, while Europe was said to suffer from rigidity, known as Eurosclerosis. In a 1999 paper that has been cited more than two thousand times, Olivier Blanchard and Justin Wolfers argued that these differences of "institutions" conditioned the responses of the two regions to "external shocks."[1] Thus the United States, with more flexible institutions, would rebound from an event like the Great Financial Crisis, and Europe would be expected to linger in stagnation.

Twelve years after the Hartz reforms, this explanation cannot hold.[2] There is today a large low-wage sector in Germany. Inequality, which was once very low, has risen. There is enormous pres-

Deutsche Welle, November 2014

sure on unemployed workers to take whatever jobs may be offered. Labor markets are therefore far more flexible than they were. No one can argue—though I suppose some may try—that the recent enactment of a loophole-ridden minimum wage has restored the power of German labor. And yet it is Germany that is dragging the Eurozone down.

Europe's economy today makes nonsense of claims that "structural reform" is the key to growth. Structural reform has been tried throughout Europe; it has produced growth nowhere. Granted, the enactments often fall short of the promises; but then each shortfall and each failure to show results sparks a call for more reforms—the true mark of fanaticism. The governments that continue to comply do so cynically: in Greece to escape (unsuccessfully, so far) from the bailout; in Italy to strengthen Mr. Renzi's EU negotiating stance.[3] Very few in the countries stricken by structural reforms delude themselves into thinking they will work.

A better place to start is the price of energy, which has been low in the United States and much higher in Europe. This is partly due to the different costs of natural gas, much more to different rates of tax. In a word, Europeans are pricing in the social costs of climate change, Americans are not. That is good for growth in the United States, bad for growth in Europe. For anyone who thinks that the markets reward virtue and punish vice, this is a most telling counterexample.

Today's falling price of oil is boosting domestic purchasing power and therefore growth in the United States; whether it will do the same in Europe depends on the reaction of households, who may spend more on other goods, or less if they expect continuing deflation. Either way, the effect is at the expense of high-cost energy producers. In the United States some shale drillers will retrench or fail, and on both continents the competitiveness of renewable energy will be challenged. For anyone who thinks that cheap oil is an unmixed blessing, the climate costs of this sudden development bear reflection.

A second key difference lies in competitive exposure to China. The United States buys from China; Germany (above all in Europe) sells to China. So a Chinese slowdown has little effect on the United States, except via the channel of lower world resource costs, which is in America's favor. But China's internal slowdown leaves high-end German machinery industries without the major growing market on which they had hoped to rely. Perhaps that will stimulate useful attention to the merits of new public investment— of a "Green New Deal" in Europe. Given the feeble proposals of Mr. Juncker in this area so far, such attention is needed.

Another key difference lies in institutions, public and financial. Despite the American reputation for having a weak welfare state, social insurance in the United States worked effectively in the crisis, sustaining incomes at the bottom of the wage-and-incomes ladder in the face of major shocks. As a result of these "automatic stabilizers," the United States was able to run very large public budget deficits and so to repair (over time) the balance sheets of the household sector. In Europe, this prop to total demand worked in the rich countries, but it was cut away by austerity in the crisis countries, and the balance sheets of both households and sovereign debtors got worse. The crisis countries are small, for the most part, so their effect on the whole Eurozone is not large. But it exists, and in those countries the conditions are catastrophic.

Finally, after years of quiet living, to a degree the American banks have now returned to their old tricks. Where before there were subprime mortgages, today there are subprime car loans and other credit delights, including massively rising student debt, which cannot be discharged in bankruptcy. These new debts have helped to buoy the American economy—for now. The risk of a later collapse, when the defaults start rolling in, is apparent, but—as always— regulators find reasons to fail to intervene in time.

In short, the United States is experiencing growth based mainly on lower energy prices, rising private debts, and an elastic public deficit—confirming Bismarck's alleged remark that God protects fools, drunks, and the United States of America.

Meanwhile, Germany and Europe suffer a slowdown rooted in weaker exports, more conservative banking practice, and fiscal cutbacks. Europe is quite right to keep energy prices high and to have more conservative banks. But this finding does confirm that if Europe wants growth—even slow growth—it has to change policies. Public fiscal austerity is the failed policy that should give way.

In particular, Europe must find a way to implement new policies of reconstruction and investment at the continental scale— including new efforts to combat climate change—and new policies of solidarity and income support for Europe's most threatened and vulnerable people, especially in the crisis countries. Especially if the whole world now gets a breathing spell from the choke-chain of rising energy costs, that would be the best way for Europe to deploy the dividend.

PART II

2015

EIGHT

The Greek Hope

Fifty-four years ago in his inaugural address, President John F. Kennedy declared, "Let us never negotiate out of fear. But let us never fear to negotiate." They were not the most soaring sentences in that short speech. But they signaled, deliberately and unmistakably to the Soviet Union, that the Cold War might be ended without turning hot, and that the world need not live forever under bluster, threat, and the fear of nuclear war.

Today, Europe faces a negotiation over debt and depression. On one side there will be the young government of Greece. On the other, the financial powers of Europe and the world. Now as then, threats are in the air.

The *Telegraph* summarized the EU finance ministers meeting on January 26: "The Eurozone has ruled out debt forgiveness for Greece." At Davos, Mr. Steffen Seibert told the oligarchs that Greece must "[hold] to its prior commitments and that the new

Social Europe, February 2015

government [must] be tied in to the reform's achievements."[1] Or as German Finance Minister Wolfgang Schäuble put it last December, "New elections change nothing."

To Greeks these comments must be a cruel joke. *What* economic recovery? *What* achievements? If elections change nothing, why bother to hold them? And of course what SYRIZA's victory drove home, above all, is the unanswerable point that failed policies *must* be changed.[2]

There are two issues: the agreements and the debt. On the first, the experiment of troika control has been tried. The results are in. Greece now proposes to regain control of its own fate. New policies to help the destitute and vulnerable, to stabilize the economy, and to foster recovery will be put in place. The past record of the Greek state is not good—this no one disputes. But the heavy-handed diktat that followed has been a disaster.

The issue behind the debt write-down is an issue of resources only in part. The problem with the alternative is that "extend and pretend" piles debt on top of debt, which is the lever that keeps the country under outside control. A write-down is the means back to policy autonomy. The form and precise terms are, in part, what negotiation is about.

The European powers hold three cudgels as negotiations start: the financing of the debts, the emergency liquidity assistance of the European Central Bank, and the fact that quantitative easing gives the ECB a new way to insulate the rest of Europe from Greece's agonies. These cudgels can be used to enforce a policy of threats, so as to maintain austerity, foreclosures, and penury in Greece.

Talks under short deadlines, coercion, and ultimatums would likely mean that Europe has decided to prevent a real discussion. If that is the decision, then the historical burden will be on those who took it, including for the chaos that may follow.

What leverage does Greece have? Not much; the heavy weapons

are on the other side. But there is something. Prime Minister Tsipras and his team can present the case of reason without threats of any kind. Then the right and moral gesture on the other side would be to throw the three cudgels away, and in particular to grant fiscal space and to guarantee Greek financial stability while talks are under way.

If that happens, then proper negotiations can proceed.

On this issue, while various northern European officials have taken to uttering dire warnings and plain threats, Chancellor Merkel has made some of the mildest comments so far. Possibly she wishes to maintain enough flexibility so as to be able to strike a deal. Possibly she understands that the choices she makes—very soon—will determine Europe's future.

In this situation, both halves of Kennedy's dictum—drafted for him, by the way, by my father—apply. Greece must not be compelled to negotiate under fear. And Europe, for its part, must not fear to negotiate—calmly, without bluster or threats, in good faith.

NINE

A Message to Sarah Raskin

Dear Sarah,

I've arrived in Athens and am installed at the finance ministry.

This message is to give you an early update on the situation.

Item. The top floor of the ministry at the moment consists of Yanis, a small team from Lazard, a secretary, and me.[1] There are deputies and others with experience, though not here on Sunday night. Let's just say that the place had to be put together from scratch in less than a week, and the job has a ways to go. The problem here is that the Greeks have to assemble both a team and a program, whereas their counterparts have an existing structure and a simple idea, which is that nothing should change, no matter how disastrous the result.

Item. The new government appears strong and united, and is hugely

Email, February 8, 2015. Sarah Bloom Raskin is deputy secretary of the Treasury. We have been friends for more than thirty years, and I endeavored to keep her and other American officials informed of the situation in Greece as events developed.

popular for now. Crossing the street with Yanis is an experience to savor: Drivers stop to shake his hand, crowds of schoolgirls mob him at the streetlights. The other day Athens saw a first in the history of the world, namely a street demonstration in support of a finance minister.

Item. The basis of the support is simple: The new government has restored dignity here and people are proud of that. The practical implication on the external front is also clear. The government will not—and in the nature of its commitments and position it cannot—buckle. It cannot give in to the intense pressures coming from Germany and elsewhere, which would like it to do what almost all other crisis-country governments have done, namely betray its voters and accept the previous terms, for the dubious privilege of staying in office a short while, morally and politically disgraced. So that will not happen.

Item. The President's statement last week was highly appreciated. There is also here (in the ministry) a feeling that the US is Greece's most valuable ally, because of the convergence of underlying interests, and that IMF is likely the second-most valuable ally, in part because of the influence of the USG and Congress over the IMF.

Item. On the other hand, local interaction with US representatives has been rough. The Treasury mission was not a success; there was an element of pedantry and condescension to their message that went down badly. The optimistic view is that Treasury was testing just how tough and determined the new team is. If so, one hopes the message came back clearly. The interaction with the US Ambassador was even worse, and got a bit hot; the feeling here was that he was hostile and very out of step with President Obama's statement.

At the same time, there is a way forward. The key policy necessity is to achieve (a) a stand-in-place framework for negotiations and (b) an end to the squeeze tactics that are producing a run on the banks, collapse of tax revenues, and standstill of activity. If these continue much longer, the situation will become irreversible.

With the European Commision the question is how to finesse differences over the elements of an agreed plan; part of the thinking here is to extend the legal shell but to identify "agreed," "newly proposed," and "suspended" provisions of the existing memorandum. Suspended policies would have to do with fire-sale privatizations and ideologically crafted "labor market reforms," neither of which have any plausible bearing on growth. Other parts of the previous memorandum, about 70 percent of the measures dealing with taxes, corruption, black markets, and streamlining public services, are much less problematic and could be considered "agreed."

On debt-sustainability the key goal is to jettison the preposterous goal of a 4.5 percent primary fiscal surplus, which was never a realistic or workable objective and never had any foundation in serious analysis. Greece can commit to a modest and realistic interim fiscal objective, along the lines of the 1.46 percent achieved in 2014. It cannot commit to a nonsense goal. Questions of debt can be resolved if the projections are placed on a plausible basis.

The essential immediate task—and it is very immediate with Chancellor Merkel in Washington tomorrow and the G-20 in Istanbul and the European council meeting Wednesday—is to buy time ("fiscal space") and to restore financial calm so that a proper renegotiation of terms can happen. A 90-day "moratorium" or "suspension" or "bridging period"—[a "suspension bridge"]—would achieve this purpose, so long as it doesn't commit the Greek government to accepting, even in principle, the parts of the previous dispensation that they cannot accept.

A bridge needn't commit the other side either, except perhaps to drop the short-term threats, which have the effect of making it harder for the Greek side to formulate their position, since it forces them to contemplate the contingency of an Armageddon that no one wants.

Long story short: this is a moment for avoiding mistakes, crisis, and precipitous action, and for buying time. Time heals. Or, at least, it gives peace a chance.

I hope this is useful.

JAMIE

TEN

A Comment on the Way Forward

The Greek government has come to Brussels to discuss the full range of economic issues with its European partners, including budgets, debt, and structural reforms.[1] At issue is whether funds will be available to keep paying the bills, on policy terms that Greece can accept.

Two factors complicate this issue. The first is the past memorandum, alongside a set of tight deadlines, created by the past government in part to entrap the new one. The second is the European decision process, which gives great apparent weight to governments of small countries, many of whom are internally insecure. The easiest path for them is to insist on no changes; anything else amounts to self-rejection.

So far, the Greek achievement consists of stating raw truths in rooms full of self-serving illusions. This exposes contradictions, bringing on facile ripostes, easily rebutted. It also brings on threats

Katherimini, February 2015

and menacing gestures, intended to test resolve. The Greek government seems to have met that test. It can now proceed to the next step.

The next step is to define carefully what may be accepted. As for reforms, as much as 70 percent of the previous memorandum is (and always has been) common ground. That which is not—fire-sale privatizations, destructive labor market liberalizations, and the unreachable 4.5 percent target primary surplus—can be spelled out. Reasonable language to describe the process of discussion to follow may be found. And the financial issues can be resolved.

When this is done, the final decision will be up to Europe. Will it continue to squeeze, in order to pressure, and so risk bringing on a Greek collapse? If so, it will be better to know that soon. But Europe may well decide, if not from pragmatism then from larger strategic vision, that Greece cannot be allowed to fail. In that case, agreement may be reached and the revival of Greece may begin.

ELEVEN

America Must Rally to Greece

As of present writing on Thursday morning, Germany has slammed the door.[1] Greece had gone the extra mile, submitting a request to continue formally under the hated bailout program, while discussing necessary changes. European Commission President Juncker was on board. But the answer came from Berlin. *Nein.*

The question was, can official Europe break out of its self-serving illusions and see the reality that is obvious everywhere in southern Europe? That reality is that the policies of the past six years have failed. They must be changed and they will be changed—with Europe's agreement or without it.

Greece has seen the most devastating failures. It has lost about one-third of GDP; its unemployment rate is 26 percent overall and more than 50 percent for the young.[2] On the avenue from Athens to Piraeus, one sees only pawn shops. Many Greeks are poor; some are hungry. That is why SYRIZA took power in Greece.

Boston Globe, February 2015

The previous government made the impossible promise that Greece could "complete" its bailout and return to private credit markets by February 28. The new government thus faced an immediate need for new financial terms. On February 4, the ECB blocked Greek banks from using state paper to obtain euros.[3] The atmosphere of deadlines and threats has set off deposit withdrawals and falling tax revenues as citizens hoard cash.

Greece therefore accepted to start discussions on refinancing and conditions. But Greece will not promise a budget surplus that it cannot achieve. It will not accept the toxic conditions of the previous program on privatizations and labor markets. It will not accept to have Greek policies dictated by the troika. Within these limits, Greece sought a bridging loan and time to discuss the remaining common ground. It was the only possible reasonable position left.

To several governments in Europe—Spain, Portugal, Finland—even this was anathema. They fear that if Greece succeeds, they will be shown up as spineless, and their internal oppositions will grow. The petty political analysis is surely correct. But those governments are probably doomed, at this point, either way they move. The Greek people have lit that fire, and it will not go out.[4]

Germany faced a choice. It could preserve the Union and the euro by changing course, negotiating in good faith, and accepting that Europe's politics and governments will be quite different next year than they are today. Or it could try to hang on to absolute power, and unchanged policies, and try to destroy the elected government of Greece and the rising opposition elsewhere, while taking its chances on the fragmentation of Europe. The disgraceful decision has now been made.

In this dramatic moment, the United States of America can step up. Greece is our NATO ally. Its new economic policy is in line with long-standing American views, as President Obama has said several times. It has shown its pragmatism and patience, its

TWELVE

Reading the Greek Deal Correctly

On Friday, as news of the Brussels deal came through, it is no surprise that most of the working press bought Germany's victory claim.[1] They have high authorities to quote and to rely on. Thus from London the *Independent* reported, "*Several analysts* agreed that the results of the talks amounted to a humiliating defeat for Greece." No details followed, the analysts were unnamed, and their affiliations went unstated—although farther down two were quoted, and both work for banks. Many similar examples could be given, from both sides of the Atlantic.

The *New Yorker* is another matter. It is an independent magazine, with a high reputation, written for a detached audience. And John Cassidy is an analytical reporter. Readers are inclined to take him seriously, and when he gets something wrong, it matters.

Cassidy's analysis appeared under the headline, "How Greece Got Outmaneuvered," and his lead paragraph contains this sentence:

Politico, February 2015

Greece's new left-wing Syriza government had been telling everyone for weeks that it wouldn't agree to extend the bailout, and that it wanted a new loan agreement that freed its hands, which marks the deal as a capitulation by Syriza and a victory for Germany and the rest of the E.U. establishment.[2]

In fact, there was never any chance for a loan agreement that freed Greece's hands. Loan agreements come with conditions. The only choices were an agreement with conditions, or no agreement and no conditions. The choice had to be made by February 28, beyond which date ECB support for the Greek banks would end. No agreement would have meant capital controls, or else bank failures, debt default, and early exit from the euro. SYRIZA was not elected to take Greece out of Europe. Hence, *in order to meet electoral commitments*, the relationship between Athens and Europe had to be "extended" in some way acceptable to both.

But extend what, exactly? There were two phrases at play, and neither was the vague "extend the bailout." The phrase "extend the current programme" appeared in troika documents, implying acceptance of the existing terms and conditions. To the Greeks this was unacceptable, but the technically-more-correct "extend the loan agreement" was less problematic. The final document extends the "Master Financial Assistance Facility Agreement" which was better still. The MFAFA is "underpinned by a set of commitments," but these are—technically—distinct. In short, the MFAFA is extended, but the commitments are to be reviewed.

Also there was the lovely word "arrangement"—which the Greek team spotted in a draft communiqué offered by Eurogroup President Jeroen Dijsselbloem on Monday afternoon and proceeded to deploy with abandon.[3] The Friday document is a masterpiece in this respect:

The purpose of the extension is the successful completion of the review on the basis of the conditions in the current *arrange-*

ment, making best use of the given flexibility which will be considered jointly with the Greek authorities and the institutions. This extension would also bridge the time for discussions on a possible follow-up *arrangement* between the Eurogroup, the institutions and Greece. The Greek authorities will present a first list of reform measures, based on the current *arrangement*, by the end of Monday February 23. The institutions will provide a first view whether this is sufficiently comprehensive to be a valid starting point for a successful conclusion of the review.

If you think you can find an unwavering commitment to the exact terms and conditions of the "current programme" in that language, good luck to you. It isn't there. So no, the troika can't come to Athens and complain about the rehiring of cleaning ladies.

To understand the issues actually at stake between Greece and Europe, you have to dig a little into the infamous "Memorandum of Understanding" signed by the previous Greek governments. A first point: not everything in that paper is unreasonable. Much merely reflects EU laws and regulations. Provisions relating to tax administration, tax evasion, corruption, and modernization of public administration are, broadly, good policy and supported by SYRIZA. So it was not difficult for the new Greek government to state adherence to "seventy percent" of the memorandum.

The remaining "thirty percent" fell mainly into three areas: fiscal targets, fire-sale privatizations, and labor law changes. The fiscal target of a 4.5 percent "primary surplus" was a dog, as everyone would admit in private. The new government does not oppose privatizations per se; it opposes those that set up price-gouging private monopolies, and it opposes fire sales that fail to bring in much money. Labor law reform is a more basic disagreement—but the position of the Greek government is in line with ILO standards, and that of the "programme" was not. These matters will now be discussed. The fiscal target is now history, and the Greeks agreed to refrain from "unilateral" measures only for the four-month period during which they will be seeking agreement.

Cassidy acknowledges some of this, but then minimizes it, with the comment that the deal "seems to rule out any large-scale embrace of Keynesian stimulus policies." In what document does any such promise exist? There is no money in Greece; the government is bankrupt. Large-scale Keynesian policies were never on the table, as they would necessarily imply exit—an expansionary policy in a new currency, with all the usual dangers. Inside the euro, investment funds have to come from better tax collection, or from the outside, including private investors and the European Investment Bank. Cassidy's comment seems to have been pulled from the air.

Another distant fantasy is the notion that the SYRIZA team was "giddy" with political success, which had come "practically out of nowhere." Actually, SYRIZA knew for months that if it could force an election last December, it would win. And I was there on Sunday night, February 8, when Prime Minister Alexis Tsipras opened Parliament with his version of the state of the union. Tsipras doesn't do giddy.

Turning to the diplomatic exchanges, Cassidy concludes that Tsipras and Varoufakis "overplayed their hand." An observer on the scene would have noticed that the Greek government remained united; initial efforts to marginalize Varoufakis were made and rebuffed. Then as talks proceeded, European Commission leaders Jean-Claude Juncker and Pierre Moscovici went off-reservation to be helpful, offering a constructive draft on Monday. Other governments softened their line. At the endgame, remarkably, it was the *German* government that split—in public—with Vice Chancellor Sigmar Gabriel calling the Greek letter a basis for negotiation after Finance Minister Wolfgang Schäuble said it wasn't. And that set up Chancellor Angela Merkel to make a mood-changing call to Alexis

Tsipras. Possibly the maneuver was choreographed. But still, it was Schäuble who took a step back in the end. It seems that none of these facts caught Cassidy's attention.

Finally, in the run-up to these talks did the Greek side fail to realize that they had no leverage, giving—as Cassidy writes—all the advantages to Schäuble once "he realized that Varoufakis couldn't play the Grexit card"? In truth the Greeks never had any intention of playing any cards, or of bluffing, as Yanis wrote in the *New York Times* and as I had written two days after the election, in *Social Europe:*

> What leverage does Greece have? Obviously, not much; the heavy weapons are on the other side. But there is something. Prime Minister Tsipras and his team can present the case of reason without threats of any kind. Then the right and moral gesture on the other side would be to . . . grant fiscal space and to guarantee Greek financial stability while talks are under way. If that happens, then proper negotiations can proceed.

That appears to be what happened. And it happened for the reason given in my essay: in the end, Chancellor Merkel preferred not to be the leader responsible for the fragmentation of Europe.

Alexis Tsipras stated it correctly. Greece won a battle—in retrospect perhaps a skirmish—and the war continues. But the political sea change that SYRIZA's victory has sparked goes on.[4] From a psychological standpoint, Greece has already changed, utterly; there is a spirit and dignity in Athens that was not there six months ago. Soon enough, new fronts will open in Spain, then perhaps Ireland, and later Portugal, all of which have elections coming. It is not likely that the government in Greece will collapse, or yield, in the talks ahead. In a year the political landscape of Europe may be quite different from what it appears to be today.

THIRTEEN

A Great German Greek Grexit Game?

Tony Curzon Price and Frances Coppola have presented compact summaries of a hypothetical game between Germany and Greece: two players, two moves, and a payoff matrix.[1] The issue between them is the structure of the payoffs, and specifically whether the "hard/hard" outcome—namely "Grexit"—is favorable or disastrous for Greece.[2]

Curzon Price is clearly right that the "game" is not "chicken." It is not zero-sum. But is it a game? Both authors overlook the strict words of Greek Finance Minister Yanis Varoufakis in the *New York Times* three weeks ago. Varoufakis wrote: "My game-theory background convinced me that it would be pure folly to think of the current deliberations between Greece and our partners as a bargaining game."

A main reason is that in the real world of Greece, Germany, and Europe the exact motivations of the players and structure of

Social Europe, March 2015

the payoffs are not known. They are not playing for chips, points, or money. And this is not a two-person game but one of shifting alliances among multiple entities with sometimes congruent, sometimes conflicting goals. It is more like the old board game Diplomacy—less a "game" than a setup for underhanded betrayals —which I cordially detested as a child.

To take first the position of "Europe," what did it know, going in, about the Greeks? Not enough. Tsipras and Varoufakis had no record in power. The internal cohesion of SYRIZA was uncertain. Would the Greek people stand up or fold under pressure? Experience foretold that, faced with pressure, European governments, no matter what their campaign promises and their internal politics, would eventually buckle to threats and toe the line.

For this reason, the initial posture of the "partners" had to be tough. It had to be tough, *even to the point of being unreasonable,* as the "sign up or get out" line of German Finance Minister Wolfgang Schäuble surely was. Otherwise, an eventual compromise could not have been sold to the Bundestag—let alone accepted, even grudgingly, by the electorally threatened Spaniards and Portuguese.

But it was also clear enough that if Greece did *not* buckle, then in the end the European side would have to give a little. Did the Greek side know this? Not for sure. But the posture of the institutional players, notably the IMF and the European Commission, and some of the governments signaled eventual compromise. The opaque inner dynamics of the German government were worrisome, like command-and-control over the Bomb. But that Chancellor Angela Merkel was unlikely to decide to sacrifice Europe merely to save Mariano Rajoy from Podemos? An easy call.

Thus while Wolfgang Schäuble could bluff—and indeed he had to—for Varoufakis bluffing could have been fatal. The opposite was required. The new Greek government had to become both *known* and *credible.* It had to demonstrate that it was (a) serious and reasonable, (b) unbending on certain points, and (c) unlikely to collapse whatever happened.

The first could be satisfied by presenting a clear program that met necessary conditions, stated essential limits, and refrained from all insincere threats. The second was met, in part, by forming a coalition with the right-wing populist Independent Greeks—a bit like burning the boats before Troy. The third was established mainly by the astonishing initial support—an approval rating above 80 percent—given to Alexis Tsipras by the Greek people.

In this way, Greece made clear that it had no "Plan B" and that it would not even flirt with the "Grexit card." If Grexit happened, the responsibility would fall on Europe. And however much Herr Schäuble might mutter imprecations, Germany was not going to make that move.

Thus a "confidence-building" act of self-restraint by Greece helped to create the climate for a similar act of restraint by Germany. And the Eurogroup came to agreement. "Constructive ambiguity" made the question of loss of face unimportant, as it is now established that neither the Greek nor the German government is going to implode over details.

In this way Greece and Germany changed the structure of their relationship. It was no longer a "one-time, noncooperating" bargaining game, but something more like a "cooperative" and "repeating" process. This does not mean that the two share the same perception of conditions or that they will agree on policies. But at present writing, they are getting down to business. There must follow detailed discussion of plans, agreements to get past funding hurdles, and measures to ensure that the Greek government does not run out of money and that the Greek banks do not collapse.[3]

Unfortunately, Germany is not the only European player—or if it is, its command-and-control remains insecure. And as John F. Kennedy observed when a U-2 strayed over the USSR during the Cuban missile crisis, "there is always some son of a bitch who doesn't get the word."

In recent days, out of motives not yet clear, the European Central Bank has acted to undermine the spirit of the short-term agreement, using tools that affect Greek bank liquidity and government financing options. Because of this, Greek finances are in trouble, the pressure remains on, the near future remains uncertain, and the policy discussions—which can succeed only if they can operate in time and quiet—are likely to be more difficult than they should be.

Surely, it is no time for such games.

FOURTEEN

The Political Level

Two things have been apparent in Athens in recent days: that the agreement reached on February 20 did not bring a change of policy by the "European partners," nor would it prove a prelude to financial stabilization. On the contrary, it is now reasonable to believe that *at the operational level*, the effect of European policy is to prevent, not to promote, an effective solution.

For Greece, the purpose of the February text was to provide a breathing space during which good-faith discussions might take place. The cost of time was concessions: previous privatizations were not reversed; a minimum-wage increase was deferred, the Greek government committed to tight fiscal targets, and, most of all, the "technical teams" of the former troika were eventually allowed to return to Athens, although under the rubric of a newly constituted Brussels Group and for fact-finding purposes only. Many observers have described these concessions as a defeat. They were, however, necessary.

Previously unpublished, March 18, 2015

But Greece needed financial help, of two types. One had to do with financing principal repayments owed primarily—at least in March—to the IMF. The other had to do with extending the emergency liquidity assistance that supports the Greek banking system. The ELA was extended, but under a tight cap that suggests liquidity might fall short at any time—and in particular should Greece fail to meet a payment on its debts.

In this way, everything came down to the short-term financing. On this, there has been no solution. By digging deep into various accounts, the Greeks managed to meet payments due last Monday. Digging deeper still, a payment was made today.[1] Next week still loomed.

Once in Athens, the twenty-four-member technical team made clear that its methods and goals were unchanged. It still sought open-ended oversight—in practical terms, control—over all aspects of Greek policy. Only after five days of meetings did the team even produce a written agenda. On Tuesday, it presented a demand for advance consultation on a revenue-neutral bill in Parliament to deal with food and electricity relief, and on another dealing with tax arrears. Fact-finding this was not.

And so on Tuesday the technical discussions broke down, although papers specifically requested will continue to flow, and a list of requests was reported to be under development as of Thursday night. A teleconference on Tuesday afternoon with the Euro Working Group was also cut short. Following disparaging statements by officials of the three "institutions," the Greek representative read a brief reply that the issue now has to be resolved at the political level—and that he was not authorized by his prime minister to say anything more.

"The political level" means Chancellor Angela Merkel. On March 16 Prime Minister Alexis Tsipras sent her a long letter that outlined the financial picture and the strangulation that is under way. The letter states, in part, that "it ought to be clear that the ECB's special restrictions . . . when combined with the disbursement delays . . . would make it impossible for any government to service its debt obligations." "Impossible" is a strong but very clear word.

Chancellor Merkel's reply was swift and understanding—though of course she made no commitments. They will meet at the European Council on Thursday in Brussels, and again, at her invitation, in Berlin on Monday, March 23.

For the Greeks, it is now necessary to fix the short-term financing issues. To stumble along until June, under all of the same pressures and uncertainties, would wreck their now very fragile economy. There are therefore just two feasible outcomes. The first is a short-term financing fix for March and for June, which will clear out the cash flow issues, stabilize the banking system, lift the cloud of default, and open the way toward implementation of the government's plans and reforms, including agreement by April 20 with the European partners as foreseen in February. The other is a breakdown now, with emergency measures coming quickly.

A decision will be needed in the next few days. It will be taken by the one person who has the power and the capacity to make it. One can understand that the choice for her will not be easy, as Greece has few friends, especially at the moment, among her supporters. Angela Merkel is, nevertheless, the leader of Europe. And so it is on her, once again, that hope for the future of Greece and the Eurozone rests.

FIFTEEN

A Report from Athens

Merci Philippe. Je suis très content d'être ici. Et, comme vous le dites, évidement il se passe quelque chose en Europe. Mais quoi exactement? C'est ça la question.[1]

I can perhaps contribute an answer to that question. I have just come this morning from Athens, where I have had, for the past several days, the high privilege of working with the government of Greece, and especially with the finance minister, my very good friend, Yanis Varoufakis. I've actually had two occasions, so far, to observe the drama that's unfolding in Europe from a close vantage point.

On March 20, 2015, I flew from Athens to Brussels to give remarks to the European Trade Union Institute, a sympathetic forum, before an audience containing numerous staff from the European Commission and other European agencies, as well as NGOs and press. The world of Brussels is padded, synthetic, anodyne; I felt it important to give a blunt account of the perspective from Athens, especially given that political enemies were beginning at that point to close in on Yanis Varoufakis. The "middle-finger" accusations were only part of a systematic campaign in the media to portray Yanis as a hot-blooded radical, which is the exact opposite of what he actually is.

The first one was during the week of the negotiations that led to the landmark agreement on February 20. And then in these past few weeks in Athens, which had their own drama as they led up to a series of payments, including a very substantial one today that was due to the International Monetary Fund. All of which had, let's say, events followed with distinct interest around the world and especially in financial circles.

What is at stake in Greece goes very far beyond merely financial questions. It goes beyond the question of the fate of a small and historically very badly governed country with weak institutions that has suffered abominably in the wake of the crisis over the past five years, losing 25 percent or so of its output. And having unemployment rates that are comparable to those in the United States during the worst period of the Great Depression, unemployment rates well over 50 percent for the youthful population, and facing severe stresses in every aspect of public and social functions.

It goes, as I say, even beyond that very grave situation, which is visible on every street in Athens and on every wall in Athens. It goes beyond that to the future of Europe and beyond that, to the meaning of the word "democracy" in our time.

But what the Greeks have done, and this is what has attracted me to become as engaged as I could be in this situation, what they've done in the past few months is astounding. They have dismantled—I think definitively—and banished an entire previous political class.

They have ended a rather rotten and corrupt previous two-party duopoly, and they have installed a government of dissidents, activists, and professors. Including, of course, a finance minister who was for years, until very recently, banned and blacklisted from Greek television by the then existing authorities. That man is now the finance minister of the Hellenic Republic.

And the Greek people did this, by the way, in the face of a wall of resistance from their own media, which continues, and in the face of a wall of incredulity from their European partners, which also continues. I would say that possibly nothing quite comparable to this has happened in Europe since the election of Solidarity in Poland at the end of the 1980s. And it is obvious that it has had a galvanizing effect on the political atmosphere outside of Greece. In fact, in many places around Europe and spreading an aspect of possibility that was not there before, opening up a window of opportunity. I believe the word in Spanish for the atmosphere that is emerging is "podemos."[2] And that is the breeze that is wafting fresh air over the entire European scene.

I have been, of course, watching the European scene with some care for the past five years especially, and the transformation, the psychological transformation, is already perceptible outside of Greece. Inside Greece it is a fundamental fact that one can observe at any time.

At the same time the new government confronts an elaborate, well-laid political and economic trap. It's more than a trap, actually. It's more like a minefield or an obstacle course that is entirely of human construction.

The trap is composed of deadlines: deadlines for reviews, deadlines for payment schedules and cash flow hurdles, that were put in place before the January 25 election, in some cases with a view toward the likely timing of that event. It is composed also of caps on liquidity assistance to the banking system, on issuance of T-bills by the government, and the ability to discount T-bills at the European Central Bank, which came into play after the election.

Each of those measures can be, and has been, rationalized as a measure of supervision or oversight or precaution. We can argue about whether that's a legitimate rationalization or not. I would have my doubts. But what one can say for sure is that the ensemble of these obstacles and, let's say, precautionary financial measures is, from a macroeconomic standpoint, from a psychological standpoint, fundamentally counterproductive. It adds materially to the instability that is perceived with respect to the Greek economy, to the instability of the financial system. It adds materially to capital flight, and to the political pressures that have been on the government and to which neither the government nor the Greek public has shown any inclination to bow.

To get past the trap, to get through the minefield, has required maneuvers of a fairly high order of adroitness in at least three stages. The first was to establish, in principle, that the previous agreement, the memorandum of understanding as it was called, which had subjected Greece to a form of colonial government according to which practically everything that the government did was dictated from outside, by the institutions known as the troika, was a thing of the past. That it was finished, that the Greek public had rejected being ruled this way in an open and decisive election. And at least in principle that proposition was accepted, after some fairly rancorous negotiations that led to the communique on February 20. This was a major step forward, although one that came at the cost of deferring certain measures in the SYRIZA election platform, including raising the minimum wage, not reversing privatizations that have previously occurred, and accepting a primary surplus target, which, although lower than the previous completely unrealistic one, is still constraining on the Greek government.

The second stage, still ongoing, involves establishing this reality at the operational level. It involves establishing a professional, acceptable working relationship between the international teams, which do have a legitimate role. That role is finding out the facts and assuring the European partners of the good faith of the Greek government. And that has required an adjustment on the part of the international teams who came back to Athens, I think, still hoping that they could conduct business as they have done before, basically under the same operational rules that had governed under the memorandum of understanding. They found out that that was not the case, and there was a certain amount of friction associated with that discovery.

I think it's fair to report that in the past several days some progress has been made. Technical discussions were suspended for a while with the proposition being that the teams would present their request for documents from the Greek government in writing. The teams are now doing that. They are working to present, perhaps as early as today, a list of documents they require, and that request will be responded to. The Greek Ministry of Finance this morning issued a statement saying that it views this as a constructive development. It's putting the relationship between the two sides on a proper footing of good order and regular exchange of documents.

A third stage in the process has to be resolved at the political level. That involves restoring the liquidity of the Greek government and enough financial stability to the banking system so that economic activity can begin to resume. That's been a major problem, especially in the past two months, in the atmosphere of fear that surrounded the election and the atmosphere of uncertainty that has succeeded it. Basically, banks have suspended most of their activity and a great deal of capital has left, requiring intermittent and rather small increases in liquidity assistance to keep the system functioning.

But that is not sufficient to allow the government the breathing space either to develop its program of reforms or to begin to open up the prospect of some recovery in the economy. A decision to move past that mechanism of destabilization had to be taken at the political level, and it is possible that that was accomplished, in part at least, last night in Berlin.[3]

Here, as was the case before the February 20 agreement, the pragmatic intervention of someone for whom I don't ordinarily offer effusive praise, namely the chancellor of the Federal Republic of

Germany, has to be acknowledged. It's a pragmatic step which may amount to a turning of the corner and an easing of the pressures from the European Central Bank.

As these maneuvers (as I call them) mature, there emerges an interesting possibility: the possibility of a politically stable, anti-austerity government in Europe, led, as I think you probably have observed, by forceful personalities, and presiding over an economy which is so far down that it has no place to go but up. An economy that may soon be on a track of some recovery, some improvement in jobs performance, and stabilization of its external debt situation.

This would be in the wake of a crisis brought on by the neo-liberal financial policies of the early part of the 2000s, and then aggravated and prolonged by the austerity ideology that succeeded the crisis, and by the profoundly counterproductive policies with which Europe has reacted to the crisis. The possibility that an anti-austerity government might lead the beginning of a recovery from the austerity regime is, I think, a present reality and it is, of course, a nightmare in certain quarters.

It is the worst thing that could happen if you are associated with the larger political system, and the larger economic policy that Europe has been pursuing. A lot of people are associated with that ideology and those policies, and you can see their reaction in recent days.

They have thrown down one last line of mines and barriers, which has been visible to everybody, and I think it deserves a word even though it is not, strictly speaking, a word about economic policy. They have begun a campaign of political character assassination aimed specifically at one pillar of the potentially forthcoming Greek revival, my friend the finance minister, Yanis Varoufakis.

This part of the game is certainly familiar to Americans. Americans of my generation have seen versions of it aimed at progressive, or ostensibly progressive, political figures on various occasions.

Gary Hart was an example, back in the eighties. Bill Clinton was an example on several occasions in the 1990s. And attempts of the same sort have been aimed at President Obama.

An attack of this kind always has two major features. One is the great principle that freedom of the press applies most particularly to those who happen to own one, which, in this case, are the rightists who own banks and media companies. The second essential element is the altogether reliable response, especially in large audiences, when references are made in public to the fact that the human male is normally endowed with a reproductive organ. Did I state that with sufficient delicacy to get away with it?

In the cases of my friend Gary Hart and of President Clinton, there were issues that could be raised. In the case of President Obama, we have a man whose visible family life is more pristine than any since Ozzie and Harriet, which is why President Obama was not taken down by this kind of attack.

In the case of Yanis Varoufakis, the attackers have essentially the same problem. Real life affords no plausible foothold, or is it perhaps handhold or a fingerhold. And so the whole thing had to rest on an alleged fleeting gesture in a long ago quasi-academic lecture.[4] The phrase for this is "scraping the bottom of the barrel."

But it is something which has been part of the political and media dynamic for the past several days, aimed in a very specific way at the one figure who has done the most to transform the political climate of economic policy discussion in the world, and especially in Europe, in the past four months. And his position in doing that was built upon a record of years and of millions of words of effective and largely accurate analysis of what has been going on.

So we need to watch and be careful not to make too little of these matters, which may seem trivial or easy to dismiss, but which are in fact intended to achieve a very specific political purpose.

This I think will pass. It will pass because the leader of the Greek government, the prime minister, Alexis Tsipras, is the real thing. I've gotten to know him, not as well as I know Yanis. But I have to say, I've met a lot of political leaders in my time and I have not known very many who approach Alexis in his ability to assess a political situation with a cool eye and make a solid judgment about it, which is why he came from nowhere—in less than four years, really in less than a year and a half—to be the prime minister of a European country.

The Greek people elected their government in complete defiance of their own media, and they have rallied behind it in the crisis that followed the election by margins that reached 80 percent, which meant that half or so of those who voted against them in the election have come to support them, at least at some point in the period that followed.

There is a spirit of dignity in Athens that is worth a great deal more than money. That's something very profound to observe. I've observed it only on maybe two or three occasions in a lifetime. That spirit is contagious and it may be felt in Spain, and it may be felt in Portugal, and it may be felt in Ireland, and elsewhere before long.

So I hope that you will not find me too portentous if I convey to you just how much this particular moment, and the chance to participate in it, has meant to me by closing with the words of Zola: *La vérité est en marche et rien ne l'arrêtera. Merci.*[5]

SIXTEEN

Does Europe Need Debt Relief?

By 1986 informed opinion understood that Third World debt would have to be reduced, written off, defaulted. The problem was to get official agreement to this fact. It was to effect a change not in thinking but in the accepted thinking. This was the contribution of the 1986 Bradley-Kemp conference, organized by Richard Medley and David Smick, which I attended happily at their expense.[1]

Today accepted thinking on European finance is centered on the Eurogroup.[2] In these meetings of finance ministers, the Greek representatives can challenge and disrupt accepted thinking, but they can't change it. Insecure politicians are bound far more by past commitments than present realities; to admit error is to concede fallibility, and to concede fallibility is to invite the thought that the other fellow might do a better job. Finance ministers have no authority to concede this. Thus the vociferous hostility of Spain, Portugal, and Finland to concessions for Greece. And then there

International Economy, April 2015

is the fact that inside the IMF and the ECB, power rests on programs, and careers depend on enforcing programs consistently, consequences be damned.

In 1986 the United States was the key creditor, and Ronald Reagan could not have a third term, so even the transition to G. H. W. Bush opened a path to change and debt resolution via Brady bonds.[3] Today in Europe it is not so easy to make a similar change. A debt conference held by the Eurogroup might achieve little. There must be a *prior* change of ideas—and some way to project change onto governments that have an inherent tendency to "stay the course" to disaster.

There are four entities whose leadership shows signs of understanding that change is now necessary. They are the IMF, the European Commission, the government of Germany (at least in the person of the chancellor, Angela Merkel), and the OECD. The problem is (in part) that in two cases that matter most, the IMF and the FRG, there is institutional inertia and entrenched ideology, and the topmost leadership exercises less than perfect political control.

The OECD, though less influential, has perhaps the greatest mental flexibility. In April, Secretary General Ángel Gurría even hosted Greek Finance Minister Yanis Varoufakis, via the annual conference of the Institute for New Economic Thinking in Paris. Perhaps Mr. Gurría, who long ago managed Mexico's Brady Bonds, might take the lead here? Gurro-Bonds—now there's an idea.

SEVENTEEN

Long-Term Strategy
Through a Realistic Lens

Memorandum—Confidential
To: Yanis
From: Jamie
Subject: Long-term strategy through a realistic lens
Date: May 3, 2015

The outline of the "New Development Model" betrays its origins in the quagmire of Euro negotiations.[1] Dominant roles are assigned to fiscal targets, public debt, and banking policies; there is even a section on "labor market reforms," and the one on state assets is to be concerned, mainly, with privatizations. To the extent that there is a growth strategy, it is conceived of as industrial growth—this sector or that one, chosen for reasons not entirely clear but possibly because they either (a) exist already or (b) are

As the negotiations wore on and their hopelessness became ever more clear, it became necessary to start thinking about the prospects facing Greece outside the euro. This note to Yanis presented my thoughts, partly in reaction to a negotiating paper he had tabled at the end of April.

part of the common culture of industrial visionaries at the moment. One may understand the logic behind the structure, but forgive me for finding it a bit dispiriting.

In truth there is no prospect for development inside the current economic structures of the Eurozone. There is also no prospect of winning change in those structures. You have tested that second prospect. But from the beginning of your government, any chance to raise the ideas of the *Modest Proposal* or similar pan-European policy change has been blocked. European strategy has been consistent; from the beginning it has been to wear you down over the months from January to June. It isn't going to change now, even if you squeak past the middle of May, if and when negotiations for a new program start. If anything, your resistance so far has accelerated the hardening of lines—a hardening that was inevitable anyway as elections approach in Spain. You are being told now to make at least one major concession to get through the next few days. In June, in my view, you will be told to stop complaining and sign up, finally, to the old program.

Let me therefore assume for the purposes of this memo that a breach is near. The point here is to look over the cliff and around the bend, and to ask: What is the long-term prospect after Greece transitions out of the euro and resumes command of its own economic policy? What can be done to make that prospect as bright as possible under the circumstances? For this purpose, let me assume (a) that the government will survive and (b) that the transition is managed without a catastrophic debacle. Neither assumption is secure, but it's not worth proceeding otherwise.

The supposed advantage of having your own currency is that it solves the competitiveness problem, so far as it can be solved, at a stroke. Those sectors that compete on domestic cost and price in international markets will be better positioned. The limitations are price rigidity and demand inelasticity.[2] Prices charged in the tourist and pharmaceutical sectors, among others, may prove rigid in euro values. Even if external prices do decline with the drachma, the gain from cheapness will not necessarily yield large gains in volume, especially in the short run. Especially not if, as with tourism, they were already doing well for other reasons. The currency is obviously irrelevant to shipping.

Preliminary inference: so far as exports are concerned, external devaluation will not prove much more effective than internal devaluation, even though it proceeds more quickly.

However, there are several advantages. The first is that devaluation doesn't produce debt deflation, since most debts go down with the currency.[3] So there will be fewer bankruptcies. The exceptions are the external debts; these will have to be renegotiated by private parties. Here the key will be to protect the debtors from asset seizures on Greek soil. Assets owned by Greek debtors outside Greece will be vulnerable; fortunately, there are not so many of those.

The second major advantage is that incomes earned at prior euro prices will translate automatically into more drachma as the drachma declines, and this will show up as an increase in the money value of exports even if nothing happens to volumes. Meanwhile, the money value of imports will also go up, but the quantities will be constrained by higher prices and can be constrained further by sumptuary taxation. So some spending that would ordinarily flow to imports will be diverted to the domestic sector. This is similar to what happened in Russia after 1998.

The result of these two forces should be an improvement in the current account (measured in drachma) and a resulting multiplier effect. If carried out in electronic payments and captured by VAT, there will be a rise in the government's surplus, which can then be offset by expanded public services, nutrition assistance, or pensions. The result will be a further balanced-budget expansion in activity. This is the third advantage.

The fourth advantage of depreciation will be a new cheapness of land, whose clearing price will probably not rise with the euro against the drachma. Cheaper land will bring in investments from Greeks with wealth outside Greece, and it should also bring in some non-Greek investments. The proceeds will then flow into the drachma accounts of the sellers, as well as into the pockets of those hired to make improvements on the properties. There should be improvement in the real estate sector, and in occupancy and maintenance of commercial buildings.

The fifth and sixth advantages will be that you and the government will be freed of the drain of making debt payments and the strain of policy negotiations. At this point debt default is largely a financial wash, since further payments would have required further loans; with nothing coming in or going out, you are at least not worse off. The end of Eurogroup meetings and of hosting the institutions at the Hilton will be a modest plus on the budget.

Suspension of external debt payments frees you on the fiscal front, up to a point. Instead of targeting a primary surplus equal to the debt outflow, you can go to a zero primary and zero actual surplus, and so pick up several—perhaps as many as three?— percentage points of GDP relative to potential. If there is capital inflow, you can go into primary and actual deficit, using capital controls to capture and redeploy foreign exchange reserves. The near-term gain overall could be four or five points of GDP relative to potential, making a material dent on unemployment while you are still young enough to enjoy it.

Once you have a debt deal, you can tighten up by a point relative to GDP. The burden of renegotiated debts should not be allowed to be greater than that, or say half of what (I gather) it is expected to be under the current dispensation over the next seven years. But a comprehensive debt settlement opens up the credit markets, so that outflow for debt service can be offset by inflow for investment.

Clearly tax and public administration reform remain key elements of the strategy; I repeat that moving to electronic payments and automatic VAT collection will do a power of good for the state coffers and the stability of the system.

At the macro level, this strategy should deliver economic growth, provided it is not derailed by tax evasion, out of control public spending, wage-price or wage-import-price spirals, capital flight, or the current account. Capital controls are anathema under the euro, but under the drachma they will be necessary. And so is currency stabilization, eventually. Once the drachma has depreciated by enough to bring money in, it should be stabilized via a swap line if one can be found, perhaps justified on ground of NATO or EU membership.[4] This alongside wage discipline should keep inflation under control so long as world commodity prices, especially oil, remain low.

As a macroeconomic posture this one remains conservative. It has no elements of open-ended public spending, such as an employer-of-last-resort scheme (as for a time in Argentina).[5] It does not rely on the Greek private sector being willing to build up financial reserves in drachma, so long as euros are available as an alternative. (If they were, the Greek public sector could run a larger deficit.) It is not inflationary beyond the effect of the initial devaluation. It is only slightly more expansionary than current policy, and so will produce only slightly better results.

But it is substantially better than the depressing prospect of a 2 percent primary surplus for the indefinite future, under a regime of endless negotiations over the precise degree and form of austerity that is required.

The long-term investment and growth program requires getting money into the country. Let me repeat that. It does not matter, and is futile to speculate, which particular sectors may have a comparative or productivity advantage and therefore be able to sell to the outside. *What matters is which sectors and which activities can attract the investment funds, from whatever sources.*

Within that stipulation, if there is any preference, it should be for sectors that absorb labor and provide employment. The Greek position in the global economy is not that of Germany and never will be. It can be close to that of Florida, or of Cuba in a hypothetical—though unlikely—well-managed future. Greece's assets are physical, human, and climatic. Its natural customers are a rapidly growing group: the world's retirees and other people with leisure time. These should now be turned to account.

Specifically, let a development strategy emphasize (a) education for the caring professions, including medicine, nursing, and personal care; (b) development of international old-age communities for year-round occupation, especially out in the countryside and on the islands; (c) world universities, combining the resources of Asia and the Middle East with the talents of American universities in a climate of academic freedom; (d) cultural exchange, artists and writers' colonies, and scientific research. Vehicles for implementing this strategy can combine tax-free zones, planning centers, and funding from both international agencies and private corporations.

In this connection, it is worth declaring that Greece should remain an economy founded on small business and small entrepreneurs, who should be protected from international corporate takeovers in sales and distribution. It should remain an economy of small shops. It should remain an economy of small pharmacies. It should protect and support its cafés, bookstores, small hotels and restaurants, small farmers, independent taxi drivers, and vegetable sellers, as well as boutiques, tailors, and so forth. This should be done in two ways. First, by promoting community-college level training and certification for quasi-professions like pharmacy—to assure that there is a supply of qualified people to keep the sector going. Second, by providing through a public bank small loans at reasonable terms for those seeking to start or maintain small independent enterprises of this type.

Explicit maintenance of these sectors should be sold to the world community as a way of maintaining the Greek comparative advantage in quality of life, and in the home space by emphasizing that it aims to maintain employment opportunities for Greeks in Greece. The explicit rejection of the high-productivity, high-volume corporate model in these areas should be a point of pride, not of defensiveness. It will have the further effect, moreover, of preparing young people for competent emigration prospects, and so help support the home economy by remittances.

Labor rights should be an integrated part of the new Greek development strategy. Here two key elements bear emphasis. First, Greece should aim to extend the scope of unionization from the public to the private sector, and especially to the workforce in the services sector, with a view toward fostering a broadly just and stable distribution of pay and incomes, via a common wages bargain. It should foster formalization of informal employment with social insurance and a fair minimum wage. This would be modeled in part on the successful postwar experience of Austria (and to a degree, Ireland), and it would aim also to maintain the competitiveness and reliability of Greek labor in the industrial sectors, so as to attract industrial investment as opportunities present.

In sum, a development strategy at this stage in the life of your government and country should aim to paint a picture of an attractive and viable future. It is not merely a document for better administration along technocratic lines. It should not promise too much, as there are limits to what can be achieved. But it needs a vision, around which the Greek people can converge. It should provide hope for an end to poverty and unemployment. It should not promise miracles, but it can and should reinforce the national sense of the value of what is already there, and it should defend that sense against the intellectual colonialism of the international institutions and the economics profession.

The point of life and work in Greece should be stability and fairness, not competition and enrichment. Those who wish to get very rich will go elsewhere, in any event. You can build a good society with the others.

EIGHTEEN

Strategic Options

To: Yanis

From: Jamie

1. From where I sit, it appears (obviously) that there is no good deal to be had in Brussels, and (more subtly) that the process of getting to a bad deal has moved into the control of others. Mysterious 89-page documents seemingly composed to the troika outline, an even-more-mysterious 650-million-euro rabbit emerging from a mysterious hat . . .[1] Both of these suggest that that process is now being stage-managed from outside our immediate spheres.

2. The fact that you (that is, Greece) were not forced to the wall on Tuesday suggests that the other side did not consider the political climate ripe. It tends to confirm that their strategy remains, as before, to wear you down to a capitulation or collapse by midsummer. You can perhaps tell the BoG that they are now in charge of pulling rabbits from hats, until mid-July.[2]

Memorandum, May 10, 2015

3. So with the next seven weeks now in view, an important consideration remains, how to ensure that the climate does not ripen.

4. Nominally, there are two tasks to be accomplished in the seven weeks: to close the current program and get the disbursement, and then to negotiate a new program on more favorable terms. Neither has any great prospect for success. The question is how best to position yourself and your resources in this phase.

5. Ideally, the PM might instruct the Brussels team—that since it is necessary to move this process along—they should now wrap up the presentation of the Greek position on closing the current program within a few days and simply return to Athens to await a decision. The less negotiating, the less the chance for counterproductive decisions.

6. But if you cannot prevent the Brussels team from carrying on, and negotiating a bad deal, perhaps the prudent thing for you to do is *to take and maintain your distance from those negotiations*, and to prepare an alternative—using only trusted resources—for the moment that the Brussels team presents its proposals to the PM. Then it will be up to him to decide.

7. The above stance would permit you to deal with an urgent priority: getting the management and operation of your ministry in good order and under good control, pending later urgent demands, including the negotiation of the new contract and preparations for possible disaster. For both of these, the more time spent in Greece, the better.

8. If it ever becomes time to move from closing the present program (the Brussels process) to negotiating a new contract (the next program), consider offering to open *your* ministry as the locus for policy negotiations on the *new* contract. This would have a number of interesting advantages: (a) it would be a concession on an irritation that the ECB complains about constantly, as my contact at the Fed has told me; (b) it would recentralize the next round of

negotiations under *your* auspices; (c) it would permit you to manage those negotiations from Athens; and (d) if they don't like the offer, it would call their bluff on the point.

9. You might even let it be known *now* that you would do this, *once* the current program is closed, the disbursement made, and a "new spirit" for negotiating has been achieved. That is, with the opening of discussions on the next phase.

10. Given the odds and the alignments, no one is under any illusions. Our assets are only the ability to think, to write, your integrity, the resolve of the people, and the hope that the cool judgment of the PM will hold up.

We can talk from Copenhagen on the 11th or 12th.

NINETEEN

A Further Message to Sarah Raskin

A note to update you on an increasingly tense situation.

Over the past days, the Greek team, including certain far-flung adjuncts, have been working flat out to put a plausible reforms document on the table. Certain parts of it are completed, including a Medium-Term Financial Strategy, a Debt Sustainability Analysis, and analyses of the labor market and pension issues. Other parts—a fuller reforms list, a brief discussion of long-term growth strategy—are constantly under development. Yanis will have a document to present, likely in the next day or so.

At the same time, the cash situation is now dire, and my information is that there are no more expedients that will get the country past the May 12 payments deadline. As you probably know, Yanis is in Paris (and, I think, Brussels) today, on a last-ditch mission, to close the existing program and get the remaining disbursement. When I spoke to him last night he did not sound hopeful.

Email, May 12, 2015

The fundamental problem here is that there are political cross-currents on the European side. The ECB appears to care a great deal about the prerogatives of its staff in Athens. The Spaniards, Portuguese, and Irish care most about their own internal political survival in forthcoming elections. The socialist parties, especially in Germany, worry about competition from their Left. All are to a degree locked into the righteousness of their previous policy regimes. And there remains a strategic view that the Greek government will either crumble or (what amounts to the same thing) capitulate if enough pressure is brought to bear. So far as I can tell, this is the same misperception that has been present since early February in those circles.

For this reason (and based only on soundings from the Greek side) it seems to me more likely than not that there will not be an easing up sufficient to meet the May 12 payment to the IMF. At that point, we move toward a state of limbo. It is possible that there will not be a formal state of default, and the ELA will not be withdrawn; the reaction of Greek bank deposit-holders is unknowable, but if they are reasonably calm, things may continue for a while as before.[1] The government could, in principle, start issuing scrip, if needed, to make internal payments.

The other possibility is that the ELA will be withdrawn, or the cap may not be increased, and the banking system may collapse. In that case there will be dramatic decisions. A possibility is thought by some to exist, which is the possibility of default and capital controls inside the euro. I do not believe the Greek government will cooperate with this, except as a transitional move.

My sense, therefore, is that the choice is binary at this stage. Either there is an agreement to provide liquidity that keeps Greece in the euro, or there will be an inexorable, involuntary move toward the exit. The two possibilities will not necessarily be resolved at the moment of a missed payment on May 12; they may move along in tandem for a while.

TWENTY

The Greek Drama and Democracy in Europe

A Nontrivial Change of Power in Greece

I had the privilege of being present in Athens on February 8 when the new government appeared for the first time before the newly elected parliament, a democratic ritual in the country from which we have inherited the word "democracy." The occasion was significant for a number of reasons.

One was that it marked something quite unusual in democratic transitions in Europe, namely the rise to power of an entirely new political formation, SYRIZA, a coalition of the parties of the radical Left, for the first time and the eclipse of what had been a long-running duopoly of power-sharing parties.

It was also significant because the opening of the Parliament was

Back in Brussels on June 2, 2015, on my way to Athens for the endgame, I spoke to the Société Royale d'Économie Politique de Belgique and the Belgian Financial Forum, giving this extended summary of the state of play. The lecture and question-and-answer session that followed occurred on the premises of the Royal Bank of Belgium. This transcript was capably prepared by the Royal Economic Society.

the occasion for the new prime minister, Alexis Tsipras, to present his governing program for the first time, an occasion equivalent to the presidential state of the union speech in the United States or the queen's speech at the opening of Parliament in Westminster.

The new minister of finance, Yanis Varoufakis, has been a colleague at the LBJ School of Public Affairs at the University of Texas at Austin. He had resigned from a visiting professorship in the first days of January 2015 in order to run for Parliament, and two days after the elections he found himself minister of finance.

When he arrived in office, Minister Varoufakis found the finance ministry rather underequipped. Its operations had to build from the ground up. The personnel consisted of the minister, two secretaries, a few advisers who had come in on an emergency basis pro bono from Lazard Frères in Paris, and an unpaid volunteer from Texas—that would be me.

On the third day after the Parliament opened, the entire government—at least as far as economic policy was concerned—which included the prime minister, the vice prime minister, the minister of finance, two ministers of state, the deputy foreign minister for international affairs, and eventually the foreign minister—were due in Brussels for an initial round of negotiations. So the government was transformed into a delegation. It came to Brussels to discuss its policies and attend the initial meetings of the Eurogroup of finance ministers. The meetings were in a way shocking to both sides.

For the European partners it was a first taste of a determined, principled, and reasoned opposition to policies that had become deeply entrenched and widely accepted over five years, and which had their ideological foundations in a line of thinking that had been only very sporadically challenged for as much as a generation, essentially rooted in a body of thought that had come to prominence in the late 1970s and early 1980s.

For the Greeks it was more like running into a brick wall: into an opposition that was rooted in suspicion, in personal distrust up to a point, and certainly in unfamiliarity. Most members of the Greek delegation had not been part of the high-level discussions before. They found their European partners to be remote from the Greek reality, and committed to political imperatives that may have been perfectly understandable but that were at best orthogonal to Greek interests.

To an American observer like myself, who had once served on the staff of the United States Congress, the initial confrontation was an initiation into the baffling improvisations of European governance, which appeared to absorb the time of high officials, principals, ministers of finance for many hours to produce documents as thin as a press release of a few paragraphs, an exercise that in most other organizations would be accomplished by staff and presented to the ministers for their signatures. The high officials of the entire European continent were absorbed in discussions of this kind to an exceptional degree.

Economic Power Devolved into the Technostructure

These two phenomena, the situation in Athens and the scene in Brussels, were closely linked. Both reflect the deeper reality that power over economic policy had effectively devolved from national governments, and also substantially from these transnational ministerial committees, into the hands of an international secretariat of mainly economists, most of them the products of the graduate education and professional screening from the mid-1970s onward.

My father wrote in a book published in 1967, *The New Industrial State*, that when power passes to the organization, it passes irretrievably. The term he coined for this phenomenon is "technostructure." And so there was, or at least to that point there had been, no real need for a policy staff in the national ministry in Athens, and none for a decision staff in Brussels. The Athens government had made no policy and the finance ministers made no decisions.

So we have to look at the technostructure and ask ourselves: What are the governing principles that determine the legitimacy of the economists' decisions, that give them their authority? This authority seems to rest on a very particular basis.

It is not and cannot be a matter of whether people approve of the decisions. In fact, economics is an austere subject and its policy recommendations—Keynes wrote about this—have for centuries been famously austere and often unpalatable. The medicine that is prescribed is often painful, and disapproval is to be expected.

Nor is the authority of these institutions based on results or evidence. Bad results may happen, but it is always possible to come up with some combination of three explanations: first, the initial conditions were worse than we realized. Secondly, the remedy was not fully applied. The prescription was good but the patient did not take the medicine. Not enough zeal. And third, we haven't had enough time. Things will get better three months or six months from now.

The economists at the helm of these international institutions are not held accountable in the same way that others are when they hold responsible positions. They cannot be compared with army officers who lose battles, naval captains whose ships run aground, politicians who have to stand for election. Economists are not ranked by the results of their recommendations. They are ranked by what one might call the a priori analytical correctness of their point of view, by their intellectual power according to the judgment of others in their profession. It's a bit like the priesthood, perhaps not accidentally. Thus they rise and fall by their constructive conformity to existing norms. There are dissidents (you're looking at one), but the dissidents operate on the margins, if they have not been effectively weeded out early in their careers.

It is not exact that failures in economics are protected or rewarded. That criticism is often made but unfair. It is that outside metrics of success or failure do not apply. A culture with this ethos, which is the dominant ethos in professional institutions—not just in Europe but also in the United States and elsewhere—was bound to have difficulty with an entity like the new government of Greece.

What had happened in Greece was something more than a crude populist revolt against the pain of economic conditions or the economic program. That pain was there and it set the framework within which you could have the political upheaval we witnessed.

Greece is a country that has suffered six years of ongoing economic decline. It has lost 27 percent of GDP, but that's just on an annual basis. Greece has been losing output for more than half a decade. It has an unemployment rate of more than 25 percent and a youth unemployment rate of more than 50 percent. It has a massive decline in the perceived quality of its schools, its public health services, the general conditions of urban life.

It is a depressing environment of closed storefronts and open pawnshops. It is a country afflicted by homelessness, emigration, and suicides. Those conditions were there, and they were necessary but not sufficient for what happened.

Quite remarkably, there also was the rise in national politics of a reasoned critique of this entire professional framework of economic thought. That was the basis of the politics of SYRIZA. It effectively forestalled the growth of influence of the extreme Right, of the Nazi Party in Greece, a development one might have expected under these economic conditions. Presenting the critique in full might be interesting, but it is not really necessary, as recent weeks have shown that it boils down to a handful of specific issues which define the differences in the negotiations between the Greek government and the European institutions.

Four Differences of Opinion . . .

The first difference concerns the overall macroeconomic posture that is appropriate going forward, which is embodied in a target for the primary surplus. A full-throated Keynesian economist would begin by asking why have a primary surplus at all when you have a 25 percent unemployment rate and your need is to create jobs: clearly the appropriate objective is a substantial primary deficit. But that is not a realistic goal in a country that depends on outside money and cannot borrow from the private markets. So the Greek government has maintained that while it is obliged to maintain a surplus, that surplus should be as small as possible. This is because a high primary surplus has a depressing effect on total output (GDP). A larger primary surplus has the effect of raising rather than lowering the ratio of the public debt to GDP. This ratio of debt to GDP has continued to rise. It now stands nominally at 180 percent under the existing policies. The highly restrictive ones that are being requested would only raise it further.

The surplus is therefore, from the standpoint of this economic critique, a *self-defeating* policy. It is a policy that is contrary to the ostensible goal of debt sustainability, which is the goal that is articulated in principle for Greece by the International Monetary Fund when it insists on the high primary surplus target.

A second difference is with respect to labor markets. Here the Greek government points out, first of all, that if you cut wages without cutting debts, you are following a well-established formula for debt deflation. Debt deflation produces bankruptcies and a diminishing rate of participation in the formal labor market. Labor market reform does not generate competitiveness. What it generates is a loss of tax base for the government and in particular of social security and pension contributions.

The result, once again, is a *self-defeating* policy in economic terms, but also one that has the character of an *unethical* experiment because there is no precedent—certainly in Europe—for the application of the very radical program of labor market deregulation that has been imposed on Greece. It is well outside the norms and standards accepted by European law and the International Labor Organization.

So the Greek position is rooted partly on common standards that exist for other countries but also and very heavily on the practical argument that the labor market policies that have been propagated are *counterproductive* from a fiscal point of view.

The third area has to do with pensions. It's set partly in the context of a pension system which, while frequently described as very generous (there are indeed aspects of it which can be fairly criticized, including very early retirements), does not maintain the bulk of pensioners very far from poverty. In fact, almost half of Greek pensioners nowadays are at or below the poverty line. That's the backdrop, but the issue is the sustainability of the pension system. Here the critical perspective offered by the Greek government is that the unsustainability of the Greek pension system is a problem not primarily of excessively generous payments but of inadequate receipts.

The inadequate receipts and contributions are once again a consequence of the two phenomena we've just discussed: the very poor performance of the economy as a whole and its depressing effect on tax revenues, and second, the informalization of the labor market and its effect on registered employment and pension contributions.

So the whole structure of problems is interlinked. Its solution requires economic reconstruction and revitalization, without which the reforms that have been pressed on Greece are utterly counterproductive.

Finally, there's a point to be made with respect to privatization. It is a simple point, thoroughly within the intellectual perspective of even the most dimwitted mainstream economist trained in elementary micro. It holds that if you put everything out for sale at once, the price falls and your buyers, recognizing the situation, do not give you very much in return for your assets. Anybody who has ever held a fire sale or a moving sale or a bankruptcy sale understands the dynamic.

So the Greek position has been that it is not opposed to privatizing state assets that cannot be effectively managed by the Greek state. There are quite a number of those that are better off in the hands of private companies, or for that matter state-owned enterprises of the People's Republic of China. The Port of Piraeus is a case in point. However, the Greek government finds that this should not be done on terms that defy commercial common sense and that do not bring revenue to the Greek state.

There's also an interesting linkage between the privatization question and the labor market question, in which you have a left-wing government of a capitalist country insisting on fair labor standards that should be accepted by a right-wing corporation from a communist country. The economic world really seems to have taken a postmodern turn.

Broadly speaking, one would be surprised if anyone really disagreed that this critique is, on its merits, incontestable. It crystallizes a larger truth, which is that further adherence to the previously established programs is an act of futility. It is this truth that the Greek people recognized in lending their support to this government. The support has gone up substantially since the election.

The entire concept of internal devaluation, of austerity in the pursuit of competitiveness, is flawed, at least insofar as it applies to the case of Greece. But for the European partners to make such an admission is deeply problematic. It requires admitting that this policy concept might also be flawed in other cases, and worse still, it would require conceding some other basis for judgment and authority in these matters than the prior knowledge and wisdom of the economists.

. . . Leading to an Out-of-the-Ordinary Negotiation Process

The negotiations, which have been proceeding for four long months, really do not have the character of normal negotiations. In the first place, there's been a strong effort to disparage and denigrate the Greek negotiation effort.

One aspect of this has been that the technical teams are overwhelmed with massive lists of questions. It would take a reasonably well-staffed government a good year of intense work to produce reputable answers to these questions—which in many cases are largely unanswerable in the first place because they deal with scenarios that are purely speculative.

Another aspect has been the repeated calls for more progress, for harder work, for more intensification but without ever feeling an obligation to offer a concrete answer or a rebuttal or a concession to any position offered by the Greek side. Progress, in other words, has been constructed by the European partners in these negotiations as not toward an agreement but only toward a capitulation.

On top of that, there has been an effort carried out largely in the press—so I'm sure visible to all of you—to delegitimize the chief economic voice of the Greek government, Yanis Varoufakis, in terms that are personally discrediting: too many interviews, too many speeches, too many travels, too much risk-taking. Then there was the "Stink-Finger" episode and finally a fuss over something that was perfectly legitimate, the fact that he recorded the finance ministers' meeting in Riga on his cellphone, something which is permitted under the rules.

All of this was intended to avoid the need to respond on any substantial ground to the points being made.

In the limit we've heard the mere fact that eighteen finance ministers lined up on one side of the question with only one on the other, as an argument for the virtue of the eighteen and the error of the one. If you take that as a principle for deciding things, then every dissident in human history, from Jesus Christ to Andrei Sakharov, will have to be disregarded for having been against the tenor of their times and therefore wrong.

An Elusive Discussion of the Economic Merits of the Reasoned Critique

Three months ago I had an opportunity to speak in Brussels and at that time what I was hoping for and urging was a negotiated solution that would be based on a reasoned discussion of the economic merits of the case. It's clear now that this was asking for too much. There really cannot be a negotiation if one side doesn't have the capacity or the leeway to enter into a reasoned discussion.

Both sides have their constraints, but I don't think there's any doubt that the constraints and inflexibility on the European side are much greater than they have been on the Greek side.

It is transparently a question of power. It's a question of establishing authority. It's a question of resentment, in part, of the negotiating arrangements that this government had the temerity to insist on.

It's also a question of its authority to insist on anything whatever. Reuters had a report some weeks ago in which an unidentified authority was quoted as saying "we must see the political pain."

That was not an economic argument at all! It indicated that the standoff is a matter of face, and the Greek government has seen this. This is why the issue has been moved up to the political level. There it is very much in the hands of the top leaders of the institutions and the one senior leader of the European political system as a whole, Chancellor Merkel.

Three Possible Outcomes

There are at this stage three possible outcomes. The first—no doubt greatly desired in some quarters—is that the Greek government might fall, either before coming to terms or after capitulating. In which case—from the European perspective—the problems go away until there is another revolt in another country, which might not be far into the future.

Yet there is a problem with basing expectations on this possibility. The problem is that—as far as I understand the politics in Athens—the government will not fall if it does not capitulate, and it will not capitulate because if it did, it would fall. So this option is not a high probability.

The second possibility is that there could be a political decision to accept or agree to the reasoned critique advanced by the government of Greece. It would be a decision to accept the possibility of a diversity of economic models in Europe. One country, two systems, is what the Chinese call it, and they've got along all right on that basis. One could ask whether a similar level of ideological flexibility is possible in Europe.

In this solution, Greece's debt would be financed or restructured inside the euro. The policy choices would—on areas of "agreement to disagree"—basically be respected. The creditors would cede precedence to voters, the Eurocrats to the national officials.

I wouldn't entirely discount this possibility. This morning in the *Financial Times* I read an article that almost leans in that direction. It made reference to the famous 70 percent/30 percent formula that one could see being a template for future resolutions: if you go with 70 percent of the memorandum, you can have the flexibility to do what you want on the other 30 percent.[1]

This second option would have an aspect of "Kadarism," a term coined after Hungary's communist leader János Kádár, who was able to develop a particular form of communism after 1956 under the nose of the Soviet Union. This is not a bad way to think about how one might proceed. I can't say I'm optimistic, because while this would be very much in the interest of the political unity of Europe and of an appropriate compromise between democratic principle and technocratic reasoning, it would be a severe reduction in the authority of the institutions.

The third possibility is the forbidden thought: a major rearrangement of the Eurozone. That is an outcome that will not be chosen by the government in Athens. In his article in *Le Monde* on May 31, Prime Minister Tsipras clearly said, "Non à une Europe à deux vitesses."[2]

It's an outcome whose very mention brings on a great deal of anxiety, especially in Greece, where people are emotionally committed to the European project, as they are in much of southern Europe. It's for that reason SYRIZA's political project was predicated on winning an acceptable solution inside the euro. It is for that reason that the Greek government has not and will not threaten an exit from the euro, but you know such a thing could come.

It's an interesting curiosity of this situation that the man who has been most responsible for framing Greek economic policy is—as is well known—a specialist in the theory of games. As such, he has been very careful, and the government has been very careful, not to play games, not to present negotiating positions from which concessions are planned in advance, but simply to spell out in a transparent and honest way where the lines are that they will not cross.

Their problem has been establishing the credibility of that position in the eyes of their negotiating partners who cannot tell whether they are playing games or not playing games or at least pretend not to be able to tell. The result is a process that gets dangerously close to major deadlines, payment deadlines in particular to the IMF this month, without—as it's now clear—there being even so much as clarity and uniformity among the negotiating partners, let alone a joint position arrived at by straightforward negotiation with the elected government of Greece.

And the expectation, based upon a good deal of European experience, is that this all can be resolved on the last day. That is a great triumph of hope over historical experience.

So the day may come, at the end of the week perhaps, perhaps a few weeks later, perhaps at the end of this month, perhaps a little bit later still, when we find a deadline that cannot be finessed and the appropriate political decisions have not been made.

In which case the path of history going forward for Europe will be really quite different from what many years ago most of us who watched the project of European unification with hope and enthusiasm expected. It will simply be different, and it will not be different only for Greece but for other countries that will surely find themselves in a similar position sooner or later if there are no appropriate changes in the economic conditions that the populations actually face.

And those changes do require accepting the need for a change of ideas, hard though it is for those of us raised as economists to do anything except carry on that which we were taught in graduate school. I'm not ending on a hopeful note. I'm ending on a note of foreboding.

But since I'm really in the territory I can remind you of the immortal precept of William of Orange at the onset of the Eighty Years' War: it is not necessary to hope in order to persevere.[3]

Thank you very much.

Questions and Answers

Would you please comment on the fact that SYRIZA *provoked the downfall of the previous Greek (coalition) government by not accepting its offer for a selection of president, and on the fact that ministers of the new government are threatening to go to another round of elections if they are forced to enter into an agreement which does not respond to the Program of Thessaloniki? How wise would that be?*

Was the decision of SYRIZA basically not to support the selection of a president by the then-ruling coalition a wise decision at the time? It was of course a political judgment which entailed a massive risk because everybody knew that the first six months of this year would be extremely difficult because of the payment schedule. And because the previous government had been offered a six-month extension of the program and has accepted only to have it extended to the end of February.

So a new government coming in was immediately under a crushing pressure to arrive at an extension. This is what happened on February 20. On the other hand, if you're in the position of being a leader of the opposition, you have to weigh that against the uncertainty of what's going to happen in the subsequent period before an election. If the election had been deferred till November of this year, who knows what the political situation would be? SYRIZA was in an advantageous position at that moment, and I don't think you can fault the political judgment on holding the election, which did result in 149 seats of the 300 of the Parliament.

On the second part of the question, having to do with part of the parliamentary caucus which is saying that they might bolt or provoke new elections if the election mandate is departed from, I think it's fair to say that if there is a significant variance from that mandate, that's what makes the left faction in SYRIZA unhappy, but under the circumstances the pressure for basic discipline inside the coalition (not just SYRIZA but also the small right-wing party that's part of the government) is very strong. Well, I could be wrong. I'm not deeply embedded in Greek parliamentary politics. It would surprise me very much if any part of that coalition fractured under the pressure. This is a situation where the pressure is actually holding things together, and if they had a larger majority I would worry more.

Fiscal austerity has created a conflict among countries in Europe, between countries with surpluses and countries with deficits. Thank you for giving us ideas for a badly needed counternarrative. Would there be an alternative approach to counter the imbalances and distorted habits of saving and investment? More precisely, should Germany not make an effort by raising real wages, reducing their surplus, and thus helping indebted countries like Greece?

This question is a very broad question dealing with the appropriate policies for Europe as a whole. This is an entirely broader topic and a question which very much resonates with the arguments by my friend Heiner Flassbeck about the source of the difficulty being the major imbalances that have risen under the euro between Germany and all of its other European partners. I don't think there is an argument: the point has a great deal of merit to it. One potential way to deal with it would be for Germany to change. Unfortunately that is very unlikely, a bit like asking the Alps to lower themselves to the level of the surrounding land.

However, as a set of steps that could be introduced into policy discussion at the European level, Yanis Varoufakis, Stuart Holland, and I coauthored a small book called the *Modest Proposal*.

The *Modest Proposal* is modest insofar as it consists only of proposals that would be possible within the framework of existing European treaties and charters. There are four elements to that proposal. First, you have to deal with the debt problems. We propose to do that using the European Central Bank as the vehicle for restructuring of debts or a certain fraction of national debts.

Second, an investment program which we propose to be done through the European Investment Bank and then combine those two and use European Investment Bank bonds as the instruments of quantitative easing. That would be a helpful way to proceed.

Third, you need to have bank resolutions at the European scale so that you don't have the problem of failing banks on the backs of governments that are also bankrupt.

Fourth, there is a set of proposals for bolstering the incomes and the position of the most vulnerable populations, nutrition assistance and unemployment insurance. This kind of thing could be done on a European scale.

Taken together, these measures would have the effect of beginning to address the problem of the imbalances. They would do so in a way that puts resources to use, either as investments or as protection of the population in the hands of the regions that are chronically in deficit, and therefore balances things out.

That is a set of measures which would buy time for larger discussion of the kind of structural change that might be necessary. It might buy political space by making the European project once again carry hope for the larger populations.

So you would have to be able to garner political support across the continent for an extension of the European project. The problem of changing things now and moving to a federation is that it is something that a European public wouldn't vote for.

So that was the approach that we proposed. It's not, however, on any agenda because it's been superseded with the election of SYRIZA and by this very much narrower and in some sense historically critical negotiating agenda that I've described in my talk just now.

Basically I totally agree with you. The major problem is that one cannot admit that mistakes have been made because Portugal, Ireland, and Spain have gone through the same kind of tightening and tough austere policy, and because liberalism as dictated by Germany has to prevail. The reactions to Finance Minister Varoufakis's proposals are very emotional and very virulent, and negative comments are made against him personally and in general against the Greek population. Would Greece be able to stay in the euro by issuing debt for internal use, that would act as a form of parallel currency? So is that a possibility given the capital flight we've recently seen taking place?

This question has to do with whether it would be possible for there to be a default inside the euro, and a parallel currency. The answer to the first part is that this would be a decision that would have to be made by the European Central Bank.

A nonpayment is not necessarily a default, because default is declared by the creditor rather than by the debtor. So if a country falls into arrears, let's say to the IMF, a certain amount of time would pass before the IMF would or would not say, "Okay, you have defaulted."

A default of that kind to an official creditor would not necessarily trigger the ratings agencies to rate Greek government bonds as being in default. They might downgrade them, but not necessarily all the way to default as long as Greece was current on its privately held debts, which it has remained. So if that's the case, it does not necessarily follow that the European Central Bank would revoke the emergency liquidity assistance on which the Greek banking system depends.

If the ECB does not revoke the ELA, then Greece is still in the euro and so from that standpoint, even without a parallel currency, it is possible to conceive of a lapse of payments even to the ECB itself that does not entail an exit from the euro zone.

That is, I think, a nontrivial possibility right now.

As far as a parallel currency is concerned, a parallel currency is basically scrip. Scrip is something which has a history in the United States, in the Depression in particular. It was used extensively by American cities. It could be used by regional and municipal governments in Europe. The way it worked was that you issued a payment, basically an IOU, which was a debt instrument, it carried an interest rate—say 5 percent—payable after two years; so something issued in 1934 could be redeemed in 1936 with a 5 percent interest on it. But the city would also accept it as payment in taxes. The effect of that was the scrip turned around sometimes just on the same day as it was issued and came back as payment of tax arrears. It was very useful and it enabled people who had tax arrears to pay them.

They would perhaps buy it up at a discount and immediately return it to the tax authorities for clearing their accounts, and it enabled the cities to continue to function, to pay all their services and their workers and their suppliers, who would accept the scrip because they too could use it for the satisfaction of taxes.

So the debt instrument became a circulating medium. Very little of it was actually still outstanding at the expiration date, and very little interest actually had to be paid as it had extinguished sooner than the interest payment was due.

That kind of model is a possibility. That would not necessarily depreciate compared to the euro, at least not significantly, because as long as it is acceptable at par as taxes, you know it would depreciate a bit and be discounted depending upon how particular vendors or retailers and so forth treated it. It might be a very useful device and it might be something which would stay within the ambit of the rules of the European Monetary Union.

Thank you for being and staying a rebel economist. I think I try to be one myself. Now, for more than thirty years, the Bretton Woods institution has imposed fiscal austerity to developing countries. This has had some rumors in Europe but not much. Now that it's much closer to our turf, we're worried. Could you comment on that, please? The second question is about the deadlines Greece faces. These deadlines look pretty much untenable: six billion euro in June to the ECB, and the same in July and in August. How do you see it going as Greece can't even reimburse the first couple of hundred millions?

It certainly is true that less-developed countries had to face austerity for thirty years. One of the interesting phenomena in the course of the past decade is that a great many of the countries which have previously been clients of the IMF paid off their debts and have been able to move away from those austerity policies. That was certainly the case in South America. They had favorable conditions for doing that, but the results in general have been positive.

Look at Brazil, where over sixteen years extreme poverty has been reduced roughly by half, and social institutions have been strengthened to an extent that was not possible before. Argentina, following the crisis, had a decade of quite strong growth. Unfortunately it is back in trouble now. One could go down the list of successes.

The result of that has been a considerable strengthening in the world of a different economic point of view. Maybe one might say partly post-Keynesian, and that is something which has not had any serious intellectual impact on Greece, but it certainly has an intellectual impact on Spain. And I think will continue to be an important fact in the economic debates going forward.

The second part of this question has to do with the deadlines, and you're right, the payment due to the IMF in June is 1.6 billion, of which 300 million is due on Friday. Then you have the major payments to the ECB that are due in July and August. Everyone agrees those payments cannot be met. There's no question: They can't be met without an agreement. So there either will be an agreement or there will be a nonpayment. That's why there's so much pressure to get an agreement done at the latest by the end of June.

So there's really nothing more to be said about that. What Euclid Tsakalotos said the other day was correct: The negotiations have merged the short-term closing of the second program and the longer-term agreement to finance through the end of the year into a single discussion. At this point it's simply impractical to keep them separate. So if a political decision is made to reach an agreement, it will probably be a two-part agreement. If there isn't a decision, there won't be a payment.

Do you think that as a citizen of Austin, Texas, if you were to learn that there is going to be an increase in the debt of the city of Austin to help finance the deficit of Chicago and Detroit, would you look favorably to such an event, with the taxes coming farther down the road to pay back those loans? This is a situation that we are facing in Europe. There is not one euro left in the till for Greece, and there is not one citizen in Western Europe who wants to increase the debt of their countries to help finance additional deficit in Greece?

On the question of whether the citizens of Austin would finance, let's say, the pensions of the citizens of Chicago, Detroit, the answer is "all the time." Because in the United States there is a federal system. In the USA we have a Pension Benefit Guaranty Corporation, and we have a Social Security System. In the US we have all kinds of ways in which the employed population of the whole country supports the retired population of the whole country.

That is very definitely the case in the United States. Now the citizens of Austin would be in the same position as you've described if it were put to a municipal vote, but it isn't put to a municipal vote. I have long argued to my European friends that we have had some experience in North America with confederacies.

The United States started out as a confederacy. We got rid of it in 1789, and then we had another confederacy in part of the country. It lasted for five years and it fell apart, well, in part because it couldn't keep its armies in the field and in part because it was a confederacy. It wasn't a federal system and so you had trouble getting the tax revenue up to Virginia, where the army was. That was a good thing that it fell apart, but we can look at it as economists and say this was part of the problem. Confederacies are not a stable economic system in a larger world.

I agree with what you said. I'm not an economist, a Belgian citizen who is not so proud of the way we handle the situation in Greece, but can we really say that it's a denial of democracy? Somehow it seems to me that it's an opposition between different democracies. Germany is as much a democracy as Greece, and then if Germany's government, or its citizens do not want to help the Greek people, so it is. It's their choice like the choice of many European citizens. So can we really say that it's a denial of democracy?

On the question of democracy: Germany is as much a democracy as Greece, but the Greek voters do not vote in Germany. So one can argue that the two populations should have equal weight. One can argue that each should have more weight than their own territory, but one cannot argue that one population should dictate terms to another. That is clearly the opposite of democracy.

As you noticed, I did not make this into a case of Germany versus Greece, which would be to echo the drama of the German press.

I made it into a description of the institutional power, which is plainly undemocratic. I'll say a word more about that, actually, because the specific case of the Central Bank is worth considering in a comparative framework.

The European Central Bank is a very curious thing: a transnational, multinational institution, with no accountability of any serious kind to anybody. It takes up and extends beyond all previous precedent the notion of independence of a central bank. The notion of central bank, by the way, is a notion which emerged initially in the United States, with the creation of the Federal Reserve in 1913.

But an "independent agency" in the United States is a term that refers to independence from the executive branch, because it's governed by a board, which is appointed for long terms. It is not independent of the government of the United States, and specifically not independent of the US Congress.

The Federal Reserve Act was written by Congress. It can be and has been amended by Congress. As a creature of Congress, the Federal Reserve has to report to Congress when asked, and I have been a staff member of the US Congress on the Banking Committee charged with designing, when I was twenty-three years old, the supervision of monetary policy. Nobody thought it was very important in those days, so it was for some kid that had just arrived from graduate school and hadn't even finished his degree, who was assigned this particular job. I was one of the people who wrote the language which is now called the dual mandate. It's amazing these kinds of things you do casually when you're practically a teenager can turn out to be major historical events forty years later, but there it is.

The basic point is that there is something quite strange and certainly highly contrary to any democratic principle, the idea that there should be an ideologically, rigidly structured central banking institution that's considered to be above any form of democratic accountability or responsibility. Anyway, harassing central bankers has been one of my pastimes all my life. I certainly don't mind continuing to do it here.

TWENTY-ONE

Notes on the Meeting, Varoufakis-Schäuble, June 8, 2015

The meeting was very cordial and confirmed for me that the two have a candid relationship, rooted in mutual appreciation. It began with Schäuble making an amusing gesture: the gift of a small handful of chocolate euros, "for your nerves."

YV then opened by saying that he had no mandate for further discussion of Schäuble's prior suggestion that they discuss a referendum that might lead to exit, and that he knew that Schäuble also had no such mandate.[1] Therefore there could be no such discussion. Schäuble acknowledged this with an air of resignation, although on this question he clearly disagreed with his instructions.

YV then stated that in his view we are heading toward a "historic failure" for which the political leadership of Europe will be

This was a private note prepared for Yanis Varoufakis on June 9, 2015, to summarize our meeting the previous day with German Finance Minister Wolfgang Schäuble in Berlin. My assessment at the end was clearly incorrect; Schäuble was hardly defeated, except possibly on the question of organizing a negotiated exit for Greece from the euro, which may have been a feint all along.

held to account, given its failure to exercise control over the institutions. The most important manifestation of this is the June 1 draft SLA [staff-level agreement] from the institutions, which was a major step backward, toward the MoU [memorandum of understanding], taking almost no account of the progress in the Brussels negotiations, and none of the red lines of the Greek government. In producing the proposed SLA, a more favorable draft from the Commission was brushed aside. The conclusion in Athens is that the ultimatum was mainly the work of the IMF, which wants no agreement without the restructuring that it cannot get from the Europeans. Hence it appears that the Europeans have lost effective control of the negotiations. Nevertheless, it will be the elected political authorities that will be responsible.

YV went on to propose a plan for ending the crisis. It is that a single set of conditions, acceptable to both sides, be agreed to as the basis for (a) closing the second program, and (b) restructuring the debt per the Greek nonpaper on ending the crisis, which would have the effect of putting Greece into Q[uantitative] E[asing] and thus restoring market access and ending the crisis. The essential elements are (a) refinancing the ECB SMP bonds through the ESM, using SMP profits to pay the IMF, and returning to the markets under QE.[2] The conditions would include a realistic target for the primary surplus, a debt brake, an independent tax authority, tax enforcement, pension reforms and other measures, consistent with core Greek positions on labor markets, low-end pensions, and privatizations. There would be no new loan money for the Greek state. Schäuble listened to the presentation at length with close attention and body language that suggested no disagreement on any point of the argument. YV stated repeatedly that a solution should be definitive and not a predicate for further failure and ongoing bailouts. It would have to be accompanied by an investment program, arranged through the EIB and elsewhere at the same time.

The most important fact about Schäuble's response was that he said, repeatedly and with a shrug, that he has "no idea" about how to resolve this matter, and "no authority" to negotiate against the preferences of the institutions. As well as no authority to discuss ways that might lead to exit. He made no suggestions and appeared to have written the matter off as a problem he has no more interest in trying to solve. It is, in other words, for Greece to manage without him.

Later in the meeting it became clear that Schäuble is also not well briefed on a significant number of factual details about the Greek economy. He did not know about the relative success of tax collections in March and April, for instance, was surprised to learn that nominal GDP in Greece was negative in 2014. He also had only a very vague (and inaccurate) recollection of the terms of the February 20 agreement. One had the impression that he was not trying very hard to stay fully informed—or perhaps that his staff work was below par. An intervention by his staff raised the issue of the cleaning ladies and of the effort to give them pay comparable to that paid in northern Europe. This too reflected limited understanding of the facts. Toward the end Schäuble resorted to some routine remarks about how the Greek government has lost credibility and lacks allies in Europe.

Schäuble seemed to me a defeated man, quite resigned—he was also at least slightly unwell and said so. The topic of an extension of the existing program—much discussed the following day in the press—did not come up.

TWENTY-TWO

What Is Reform?

The Strange Case of Greece and Europe

On our way back from Berlin on Tuesday, Greek Finance Minister Yanis Varoufakis remarked to me that current usage of the word "reform" has its origins in the middle period of the Soviet Union, notably under Khrushchev, when modernizing academics sought to introduce elements of decentralization and market process into a sclerotic planning system.[1] In those years, when the American struggle was for rights and some young Europeans still dreamed of revolution, "reform" was not much used in the West. Today, in an odd twist of convergence, it has become the watchword of the ruling class.

The word "reform" has now become central to the tug of war between Greece and its creditors. New debt relief might be possible —but only if the Greeks agree to "reforms." But what reforms and to what end? The press has generally tossed around the word as if there were broad agreement on its meaning.

American Prospect, June 12, 2015

The specific reforms demanded by Greece's creditors today are a peculiar blend. They aim to reduce the state; in this sense they are "market-oriented." Yet they are the furthest thing from promoting decentralization and diversity. On the contrary, they work to destroy local institutions and to impose a single policy model across Europe, with Greece not at the trailing edge but actually in the vanguard. In this other sense the proposals are totalitarian—though the philosophical father is Friedrich von Hayek, the political forebear, to put a crude point on it, is Stalin.

Modern Europe's version of market Stalinism, so far as it affects Greece, has three main prongs. The first concerns pensions, the second labor markets, and the third privatizations. Then there is an overarching question of taxes, austerity, and debt sustainability, to which we can come back later.

With respect to pensions, the creditors demand that about one percent of GDP be cut *this year* from pension payments, in a country where almost half of pensions deliver sums below the poverty line. The specific demand would cut about 120 euros from pensions at the level of 350 euros or less per month. The government replies that while the pension system requires reform—the present early retirement age is unsustainable—that reform can be done only gradually and alongside the introduction of an effective unemployment insurance scheme.

On labor markets, the creditors have already imposed the near-complete elimination of collective bargaining and reduction of minimum wages. The government points out that the effect is to informalize the labor market, so that labor is not registered and pension contributions are not paid, which in turn undermines the pension system. The Greek proposal is to design a new collective bargaining system that meets the standards of the International Labor Organization.

As for privatization, the creditors have demanded the sale of airports, seaports, and electric utilities, among other assets, and that all this be done quickly. Here the Greek objection is not to private or foreign management of certain assets but rather against letting them go for cheap, or without conditions, or without retaining an equity stake. Thus in the ongoing privatization of the port of Piraeus to the Chinese firm Cosco, the government has insisted on an investment plan and on labor rights.

Turning to taxes, the creditors have demanded a hefty increase in the value-added tax—which already has a top rate of 23 percent. Among other things, the burden would fall on medicines (and therefore on the elderly) and on the special rates enjoyed by the Greek islands (about 10 percent of the country by population), where tourism is centered and where costs are higher in any event. The government points out that tax increases on tourism hurt competitiveness, and that the overall effect of the increased tax burden will be to reduce activity, worsening the debt problem. What is needed, instead, is tax enforcement; reducing VAT evasion could, quite readily, permit rates to be lowered.

What is missing from the creditors' demands is, well, *reform.* Cuts in pensions and VAT increases are not reform; they add nothing to economic activity or to competitiveness. Fire-sale privatization can lead to predatory private monopolies, as anyone living in Latin America or Texas knows. Labor market deregulation is in the nature of an unethical experiment, the imposition of pain as therapy, something the internal records of the IMF as far back as 2010 confirm. No one can suggest that wage cuts can bring Greece into effective competition for jobs in traded goods with either Germany or Asia. Instead, what will happen is that anyone with competitive skills will leave.

Reform in any true sense requires time, patience, planning, and money. Pension reform and social insurance, modern labor rights, sensible privatizations, and effective tax collection are reforms. So are measures relating to public administration, the justice system, tax enforcement, statistical integrity, and other matters, which are agreed in principle and which the Greeks would implement readily if the creditors would permit it—but for negotiating reasons they do not permit it. Other reforms would include an investment program emphasizing the advanced services Greece is well suited to provide, including in health care, elder care, higher education, research, and the arts. Reform requires recognizing that Greece cannot succeed by being the same as other countries; it must be different—a country with small shops, small hotels, high culture, and open beaches. A debt restructuring that would bring Greece back to the markets (and yes, that could be done, and the Greeks have a proposal to do it) would also be, on any reasonable reckoning, a reform.

The plain object of the creditors' program is therefore *not* reform. It is the doubling-down on debt collection in the face of disaster. Pension cuts, wage cuts, tax increases, and fire sales are offered up on the magical thought that the economy will recover *despite* the burden of higher taxes, lower purchasing power, and external repatriation of profits from privatization. This magic has been tested for five years with no success. That is why, instead of recovering as predicted after the bailout of 2010, Greece has suffered a loss of over 25 percent of its income with no end in sight. That is why the debt burden has gone from about 100 percent of GDP to 180 percent. But to admit this failure in the case of Greece would be to undermine the entire European policy project and the authority of those who run it.

So the Greek talks remain at a stalemate. Actually, it is not quite a stalemate, since the Greeks are under extreme pressure. Either they concede to the creditors' positions, or they may find their banks closed and themselves forced out of the euro, with highly disruptive consequences, at least in the short run. The creditors know this. So they keep backing the Greeks toward a wall—never changing their own position while complaining that the *Greek* side isn't working hard enough. And as the Greeks yield ground, inch by inch, the creditors simply press for more.

It is the ugly dynamic of negotiation under duress, between a strong party and a weak one, in this case complicated by the fact that the creditor side has no unified leadership, and hence no one—unless Angela Merkel finally steps forward to take up the role—who can make reasonable concessions and force through an acceptable deal. So the choices narrow. Either the Greek government will concede too much, lose its support, and collapse—in which case, whether the end result is another receivership or Golden Dawn, democracy is dead in Europe. Or, in the end, the Greeks will be forced to take their fate—at enormous risk and cost—into their own hands, and to hope for help from wherever it might come.

TWENTY-THREE

What Can Happen in the Next Days?

To define you and your commitment in Greek situation: Professor James Galbraith is a good friend and counsellor of Greece Finance Minister Yanis Varoufakis. He's one of the economists of the "anti-austerity party" (very thin in the EU, much larger in the US), on the ground that the choice to restrain public demand in times on economic turndown is a suicidal choice.

Good.

What can happen in next days in Greece? Will the people be able to vote? Eurogroup refused to extend the financial assistance program until the vote, so do you think that referendum still makes sense, or in the next days will the situation precipitate panic, liquidity crisis, financial turmoil, or even social turmoil?

I think the vote will occur, and the question will be clear enough to most Greeks that it will be a legitimate referendum. There is a

A brief interview with the Italian journalist Roberta Carlini, published July 1, 2015, in *Messagero* and other Italian papers. The reference to the "Next Days" is to the referendum on the terms of the memorandum, which had been called on June 27 by Alexis Tsipras for July 5.

certain amount of anxiety apparent in Greece today, but supplies on hand are adequate, and it may be that the atmosphere will calm down rather than blow up in the days ahead. We shall see.

What do you think would be the alternative scenarios if the "yes" wins? And if the "no" wins?

In the case of "yes," the government will go back to the creditors and accept their proposals. In the case of "no" they will again go back, having made clear that they cannot accept the proposals. What will happen then will be decided in the other capitals of Europe and at the IMF.

Today Juncker appealed directly to Greek people, asking them to vote "yes." Juncker is not very popular in Greece. . . . A good (accidental) help for Tsipras, or the opposite?

I doubt that the voice of Jean-Claude Juncker carries very far in Greece.

People tend to associate default with the exit from Eurozone: Is that unavoidable? And in that case, will the Greece remain in the EU?

Default to the IMF is not synonymous with exit from the Eurozone. It will of course expose further the folly of IMF participation in the Greek bailout in the first place, and the inept decisions of the IMF's managing directors from Dominique Strauss-Kahn forward, colored in certain cases by their own political ambitions and certainly not related to the best interest of Greece. There is also no mechanism under the treaties that can compel Greece to exit the EU.

Europeans seem to be less worried by geopolitical scenario than Americans: Can Greece really become Putin's Trojan horse in Europe?

No, of course not.

"They were so close to an agreement. . . ." Many reconstructions of the last dramatic hours of the negotiation tell us that the agreement was very close, and the breakdown came on a very little difference over the final VAT rates. If it's true, how can it have happened?

It is true that the Greek side had presented offers that met the creditors' demands for continuing austerity; they declined only to put the primary burden on the elderly and poor. Greece expected that "equivalent measures" would be acceptable, based on past experience of other countries and representations received only recently. But the creditors insisted on what was very close to full implementation of the MoU, and they hardened their position, apparently under pressure from the IMF, at the last minute. Also, debt restructuring had not been discussed. So it is meretricious to say that there was a near-agreement.

In case of Grexit, do you think that financial speculation will soon move to other countries, like Italy, Spain, Portugal, or will Draghi's firewall work?

An irony of this situation is that the European Central Bank is using its enormous power to stabilize Italy, Spain, and Portugal while at the same time it has destabilized Greece. This is obvious to everyone, and so I expect that ultimately the next threat to the Eurozone would come from political rebellion rather than financial speculation. I do not think that rebellion can be quelled by making an example of the Greeks.

TWENTY-FOUR

Bad Faith

The IMF and Europe on Greece

Readers of the financial press may be forgiven for thinking that the negotiations between Greece and Europe have one feckless partner—the new government of Greece—and one responsible partner, a common front of major governments and creditor institutions, high-minded in their pursuit of rational policies and the common European interest.

The view from Athens is different. On June 11, I attended the hearing of a Greek parliamentary commission investigating the Greek debt. Phillipe Legrain, former adviser to the then-EU president José Manuel Barroso, testified. Legrain is a technocrat, an economist, and a very reserved individual. He spoke in measured tones.

The original crime in the Greek affair, Legrain said, was committed in May 2010, when it became clear that the country was insolvent. At that time, the IMF staff was convinced that Greek debts

Project Syndicate, June 2015

must be restructured, and that debt relief was not only necessary but also just, given that reckless borrowers are always matched to reckless lenders, and that lenders are compensated, in part, for the risk of loss.

Restructuring did not happen. Instead, a trio of Frenchmen—at the IMF, at the European Central Bank, and at the Élysée, and backed by Angela Merkel—decided to pretend that Greece's problem was merely temporary, that there was a larger financial crisis to be warded off, and that the largest bailout in history should be directed not to save Greece but to offload the exposure of French and German banks onto all the European states, with Germany's taxpayers taking the largest share.

Why did the IMF get into the act, making its largest loan in history (thirty-two times Greece's quota) over the reservations of its staff and the objections of many non-European members? Because the managing director at the time, Dominique Strauss-Kahn, wanted to become president of France.

At the same time, the European Central Bank under Jean-Claude Trichet bought up some twenty-seven billion euros in Greek bonds, thereby raising their price. Why did Trichet do this? To support the original lenders, once again in large part the French banks.

In so doing, the European powers were able to avoid imposing losses on the large banks. And by his actions, Trichet locked the ECB into a refusal to accept losses on Greek bonds as he stretched, if not broke, the legal mandate of the European Central Bank.

As a basic principle of finance: *You do not make new loans to a bankrupt.* What you do, when faced with insolvency, is *restructure the debt.* IMF staff and board members who understood this at the time were overruled. Instead, the leadership of Europe joined in an enormous lie: the pretense that the Greek debt could be sustained. In 2010, the IMF representatives of France, Germany, and the Netherlands promised (on that pretense) that their banks would hold on to their Greek debts. In fact, they sold off everything they could.

Back in 2010, the Greek government could have restructured its own debt, under Greek law, but it failed to do so. When a restructuring did occur in 2012, it was on the creditors' terms, which was why Greek pension funds lost 60 percent of their value. And that, of course, is a major reason why Greek pensions are in such terrible trouble today.

In 2010 Greece had to swallow an austerity program that would be—as Poul Thomsen of the IMF promised the IMF Board—"tough, difficult, and painful." Although the program called for an unprecedented "fiscal adjustment" of 16 percent of GDP, it also predicted that Greece would suffer a fall of GDP on the order of only 5 percent, to be followed by recovery beginning in 2013. Meanwhile the debt-to-GDP ratio would rise to 150 percent by 2013 and decline thereafter. In fact, the fall in Greek GDP was *five times* as large, the debt-to-GDP ratio today stands above 180 percent. And there has been no recovery at all.

Later in the hearing, Legrain was asked his view of the economists behind these predictions and the officials who voiced them. On this one point, his testimony faltered. Was it incompetence? Panic? Ideology? The witness was unsure. Perhaps, he offered, some of them, "in their stupidity," thought it was going to work. In any event, as he testified, "nobody has suffered for their mistakes."

No. Mr. Thomsen continues to call the shots at the IMF, which—although it now argues the need for debt relief—continues to demand the same package of deflationary cuts that pass in official language as "reforms." Among these are savage reductions in the lowest pensions Greece pays, which would cut a third from payments that are already only about twelve euros per day.

Meanwhile, according to a report in the Frankfurt *Allgemeine Zeitung* on June 14, the European commission was prepared to lighten up on those pension cuts in return for cuts in the Greek military budget. Who torpedoed this? According to the *Allgemeine Zeitung*, it was the IMF. If members of that agency believe that it will be easier to pressure the Greek government to starve its elderly poor, they truly have not been paying attention. Or, more likely, given the now-clear divisions and disarray among the creditors, the IMF has decided that it does not want any agreement—and therefore further negotiations are futile.

And as the IMF insists that Greece meet every condition, things are quite different just a bit to the north and east. For Ukraine, according to a statement by Mme. Lagarde on June 12, as reported by Zero Hedge, the IMF "could lend to Ukraine even if Ukraine determines it cannot service its debt."[1] So much for debt sustainability—for the bedrock principle that you *do not make new loans to a bankrupt.*

Sympathetic American readers have become used to seeing Germany, the Germans, Chancellor Angela Merkel, and her finance minister, Wolfgang Schäuble, as the villains in this drama. They have underestimated the half-hidden role of the Rasputins of Paris. And also that of the Svengali of Frankfurt, Mario Draghi, who as I write rumbles threats to the Greek banking system. These are threats that may, in the next few days, unleash the very avalanche that Draghi once promised to do *whatever it takes* to prevent.

TWENTY-FIVE

Only the "No" Can Save the Euro

Greece is heading toward a referendum on Sunday on which the future of the country and its elected government will depend, and with the fate of the euro and the European Union also in the balance. At present writing, Greece has missed a payment to the IMF, negotiations have broken off, and the great and good are writing off the Greek government and calling for a "yes" vote, accepting the creditors' terms for "reform," in order to "save the euro."[1] In all of these judgments, they are, not for the first time, mistaken.

To understand the bitter fight, it helps first to realize that the leaders of today's Europe are shallow, cloistered people, preoccupied with their local politics and unequipped, morally or intellectually, to cope with a continental problem. This is true of Angela Merkel in Germany, of François Hollande in France, and it is true also of Christine Lagarde at the IMF. In particular northern Eu-

American Prospect, July 1, 2015

rope's leaders have not felt the crisis and do not know the economics, and in both respects they are the direct opposite of the Greeks.

For the northern Europeans, the professionals at the "institutions" set the terms, and there is only one possible outcome: to conform. The allowed negotiation was of one type only: more concessions by the Greek side. Any delay, any objection, could be seen only as posturing. Posturing is normal of course; politicians expect it. But to his fellow finance ministers the idea that the Greek Finance Minister Yanis Varoufakis was *not* posturing did not occur. When Varoufakis would not stop, their response was loathing and character assassination.

Contrary to some uninformed commentary, the Greek government knew from the beginning that it faced fierce hostility from Spain, Portugal, and Ireland, deep suspicion from the mainstream left in France and Italy, implacable obstruction from Germany and the IMF, and destabilization from the European Central Bank. But for a long time, these points were not proved internally. There are influential persons close to Tsipras who did not believe it. There are others who felt that, in the end, Greece would have to take what it could get. So Tsipras adopted a policy of giving ground. He let the accommodation caucus negotiate. And as they came back with concession after concession, he winced and agreed.

Ultimately, the Greek government found that it had to bow to the creditors' demands for a large and permanent primary surplus target. This was a hard blow; it meant accepting the austerity that the government had been elected to reject. But the Greeks did insist on the right to determine the form of austerity, and that form would be mainly to raise taxes on the wealthiest Greeks and on business profits. At least the proposal protected Greece's poorest pensioners from further devastating cuts, and it did not surrender on fundamental labor rights.

The creditors rejected even this. They insisted on austerity and also on dictating its precise shape. In this they made clear that they would not treat Greece as they have any other European country. The creditors tabled a take-it-or-leave-it offer that they knew Tsipras could not accept. Tsipras was on the line in any case. He decided to take his chances with a vote.

The stunned and furious reaction of the European leaders was, possibly, not entirely inauthentic. Perhaps they did not realize they were dealing with something not seen in Europe for some years: a political leader. Alexis Tsipras has been on the international stage for only a few months. He is brash, but charming. It would be easy for those as sheltered as Europe's present leaders to fail to figure him out—to fail to realize that like Varoufakis, Tsipras meant what he said.

Faced with Tsipras's decision to call a referendum, Merkel and her deputy chancellor, Sigmar Gabriel, Hollande of France, and David Cameron of Britain—and shamefully also Italy's Matteo Renzi—all sent direct messages to the Greek people, that they would really be voting on membership in the euro. European Commission President Jean-Claude Juncker went further, saying that it would be a vote on membership in the *European Union*. It was an orchestrated threat: Surrender or else.

In fact, neither the euro nor the EU is at issue. The plain language of the referendum states that the vote is about the creditors' terms. The threat to expel Greece is an obvious bluff. There is no legal way to eject Greece from the Eurozone or the EU. The referendum is actually, and obviously, on the survival of the elected government in Greece. The European leaders know this, and they are trying now to ensure that Tsipras falls.

What does Tsipras gain by a "no" vote? Apart from political survival, only this: it is his way of proving, once for all, that he cannot yield to the conditions being demanded. So then the onus will be back on the creditors, and if they choose to destroy a European country, the crime will on their hands for all to see.

That said, there is no guarantee that Tsipras will win on Sunday. In the January elections, his party won only 40 percent; now he needs a majority. Fear and confusion abound. The Greeks are, in effect, voting for a choice of unknowns, which can never be a sure thing.

If the Greeks vote "no," there is obvious uncertainty over the economic future. Perhaps the banks will stay shut, the deposits will be lost, and the creditors will carry through their threats. The uncertainty is amplified, unavoidably, by the fact that the government cannot campaign to stay in the euro and also explain how it would handle the trauma of being forced out. If there have been preparations, they are a well-kept secret so far.[2]

If the Greeks vote "yes," on the other hand, the uncertainty is political. SYRIZA may split and its government may fall. What then? There is no credible alternative government in Greece. Moreover, it is hard to think that *any* government formed to accept the surrender and deepen the depression would last very long.

And it seems certain that after a "yes," a surrender, and a deeper depression, the official opposition would no longer be the pro-European Left that is today's government in Greece. Europe will have destroyed that. The new opposition, and someday the government, will be either a left or a right party opposed to the euro and to the Union. It could be Golden Dawn, the neo-Nazi party. The lesson of Greece also will not be lost on oppositions elsewhere, including the rising far right in France.

The irony of the case is that the true hope—the only hope—for Europe lies in a "no" vote on Sunday, followed by renewed negotiations and a better deal. "Yes" is a vote for fear, against dignity and independence. Fear is powerful—but dignity and independence have a way of coming back.

TWENTY-SIX

Nine Myths About the Greek Referendum

The citizens of Greece face a referendum Sunday, July 5, that could decide the survival of their elected government and the fate of the country in the Eurozone and Europe. Narrowly, they're voting on whether to accept or reject the terms dictated by their creditors last week. What's it really about? I have had a close view of the process, from both the United States and Athens, after working for the past four years with Yanis Varoufakis, now the Greek finance minister. I've come to realize that there are many myths in circulation about this crisis; here are nine that Americans should see through.

1. The referendum is about the euro.

As soon as Greek Prime Minister Alexis Tsipras announced the referendum, François Hollande, David Cameron, Matteo Renzi, and the German deputy chancellor, Sigmar Gabriel, told the Greeks that

Politico, early July 2015; the *Politico* site does not record the exact date of publication.

a "no" vote would amount to Greece leaving the euro. Jean-Claude Juncker, president of the European Commission, went farther: he said "no" means leaving the *European Union*. In fact, the Greek government has stated many times that—yes or no—it is irrevocably committed to the Union and the euro. And legally, according to the treaties, Greece cannot be expelled from either.

2. The IMF has been flexible.

IMF Managing Director Christine Lagarde claims that her institution has shown "flexibility" in negotiations with the Greeks. In fact, the IMF has conceded almost nothing over four months: not on taxes, pensions, wages, collective bargaining, or the amount of Greece's debt. Greek chief negotiator Euclid Tsakalatos circulated a briefing on the breakdown that gives details, and concludes: "So what does the Greek government think of the proposed flexibility of the Institutions? It would be a great idea."

3. The creditors have been generous.

Angela Merkel has called the terms offered by the creditors "very generous" to Greece. But in fact the creditors have continued to insist on a crushing austerity program, predicated on a target for a budget surplus that Greece cannot possibly meet, and on the continuation of draconian policies that have already cost the Greeks more than a quarter of their income and plunged the country into depression. Debt restructuring, which is obviously necessary, has also been refused.

4. The European Central Bank has protected Greek financial stability.

A central bank is supposed to protect the financial stability of solvent banks. But from early February, the ECB cut off direct financing of Greek banks, instead drip-feeding them expensive liquidity on special "emergency" terms. This promoted a slow run on the banks and paralyzed economic activity. When the negotiations broke down the ECB capped the assistance, prompting a fast bank run and giving them an excuse to impose capital controls and effectively shut the banks down.

5. The Greek government is imperiling its American alliance.

This is a particular worry of some US conservatives, who see a leftist government in power and assume that it is pro-Russian and anti-NATO. It is true that the Greek left has historic complaints against the United States, notably for CIA support of the military junta that ruled from 1967 to 1974. But in fact, attitudes on the Greek left have changed, thanks partly to experience with the Germans. This government is pro-American and firmly a member of NATO.

6. Alexis Tsipras called the IMF a "criminal" organization.

That was, charitably, an overheated headline slapped by Bloomberg onto a very moderate parliamentary speech, which correctly pointed out that the IMF's economic and debt projections for Greece back when austerity was first imposed in 2010 were catastrophically optimistic. In fact, every letter from Tsipras to the creditors has been couched in formal and respectful language.

7. The Greek government is playing games.

Because Finance Minister Varoufakis knows the economic field called game theory, lazy pundits have for months opined that he is playing "chicken" or "poker" or some other game. In Heraklion two weeks ago, Varoufakis denied this, as he has done many times: "We're not bluffing. We're not even *meta-bluffing.*" Indeed there are no hidden cards. The Greek red lines—the points of principle on which this government refuses to budge, on labor rights, against cuts in poverty-level pensions and fire-sale privatizations—have been in plain view from day one.

8. A "yes" vote will save Europe.

"Yes" would mean more austerity and social destruction, and the government that implements it cannot last long. The one that follows will not be led by Alexis Tsipras and Yanis Varoufakis—the last leaders, perhaps anywhere in Europe, of an authentic pro-European Left. If they fall, the anti-Europeans will come next, possibly including ultraright elements such as the Greek Nazi party, Golden Dawn. And the anti-European fire will spread, to France, the UK, and Spain, among other countries.

9. A "no" vote will destroy Europe.

In fact, only the "no" can save Greece—and by saving Greece, save Europe. A "no" means that the Greek people will not bend, that their government will not fall, and that the creditors need, finally, to come to terms with the failures of European policy so far. Negotiations can then resume—or more correctly, proper negotiations can then start. This is vital, if Europe is to be saved. If there ever was a moment when the United States should speak for decency and democratic values—as well as our national interest—it is right now.

TWENTY-SEVEN

What Is the Matter with Europe?

A modern hospital is equipped with a variety of specialized wards. One of them is the intensive care unit, or ICU. Here go those who are especially sick and in need of the most devoted attention. The existence of the ICU recognizes that illness and operations do not affect all patients in the same way. Some, who are robust, recover quickly. Others who are weaker or older or sicker may require different treatments and more help.

Europe's financial hospital has been busy for five years, dealing with victims of the world crisis and of the lending binge that came before it. Ireland, Portugal, Spain, and (to a degree) Italy have filled the beds. They have taken the medicine and followed the prescribed routine. Not one has fully recovered. But then again, none of those countries were ever *lethally* sick—at the worst, they suf-

American Prospect, June 2015. This piece was written just in advance of the July 5 referendum that marked the climax of the Greek crisis.

fered declines of 5 to 10 percent of GDP and have been more or less stable for the past few years.

Greece is a special case. She was a weak patient to begin with. Her institutions were not strong. Her industries were not competitive. She did binge on those precrisis loans. And when the collapse came, Europe and the IMF prescribed an exceptional dose of the standard drugs—perhaps three times more than was given to anyone else. The results were toxic. Greece has lost more than a quarter of her income, she has 29 percent unemployment, and her government has no cash reserves.

In any modern hospital, this patient would be on life support. Transfusions would be given. Intravenous hydration, a feeding tube, and an oxygen mask would be supplied. The doctors would not be embarrassed; on the contrary, they expect that in certain cases, the routine treatments do not work. They expect that in certain cases, more is required.

But today's Europe is a hospital with no ICU. Instead, the doctors have kept the patient in the ordinary ward. Every few days, they come in and check the charts. They see that there has been no change. And so they lecture the patient. She must exercise! She must take still more of the medicine! She must not expect special treatment! After all, they point out, look at the other patients! See how much better *they* are doing! And on and on. And then the doctors depart.

Meanwhile, back in their offices, the doctors feud. One—the IMF—says that surgery is essential, to restructure the patient's debt. Others—from the governments of Germany and other states —object that such surgery is costly and they do not wish to pay the bill. Meanwhile, the European Central Bank administers saline liquidity—drip by drip—to the patient's banks.

After five years of this, with death in sight, the Greek people have decided to reject the treatments.[1] They have asked, over the past four months, for meetings with the hospital directors, to see whether the protocols can be changed. They have been told, no, not unless your doctors agree. But the doctors do not like to have their authority challenged. And just imagine—they report back to their chiefs—what would happen if we agreed? Soon the other patients might get ideas; think of what that would cost! So the treatments remain the same and the results get worse.

There is a principle here, and it is, in origin, incontestably Greek. The principle is "First, do no harm." Has that principle now been replaced by another, originating in the sordid culture of international finance: "First, lose no money?"

And if so, should the patient leave the hospital? That is the choice she now must face. It is not an easy choice. If you go home, you may die. The doctors do not want you to leave. They place obstacles in the way. To defy them requires real courage, as anyone who has ever been in the situation knows.

But then again, maybe back home, things will improve? Maybe that debt can just be cut off—a crude operation that sometimes does save lives. Maybe the fresh air and home cooking will help? Imagine how furious those doctors will be when they see the patient getting better on her own!

That is where we are, dear friends, in the struggle between Greece, Europe, and the IMF. The outcome cannot be known, and in the end, History will judge. But I believe that when History does judge these matters, sympathy will be with the patient Greece. Committees of squabbling doctors, jealous of their power and stuck in their ways, do not come off well.

TWENTY-EIGHT

Exit Made Easy

Yanis, in your essay in the *Guardian* today you write:

> To exit, we would have to create a new currency from scratch. In occupied Iraq, the introduction of new paper money took almost a year, 20 or so Boeing 747s, the mobilisation of the US military's might, three printing firms and hundreds of trucks. In the absence of such support, Grexit would be the equivalent of announcing a large devaluation more than 18 months in advance: a recipe for liquidating all Greek capital stock and transferring it abroad by any means available.

This reflects expert opinion and also our internal discussions. But I'm increasingly convinced that we were looking at the problem wrongly; that we failed to assemble the puzzle pieces in a cor-

Private message, July 10, 2015. Yanis Varoufakis resigned as finance minister on the morning of July 6, and I returned to the United States on the following day. This note to Yanis was based on reflections on the days immediately afterward.

rect manner. This purely private note is an effort to spell out and refine my thinking.

To begin with, the Iraq analogy is invalid. Iraq was a destroyed country with an all-cash economy, physically damaged infrastructure, no internal transport system, no internal security, and no banking system. Greece is none of those things, and it would not need the US military or even the Greek military to do the job. The key in Greece is to use the existing systems effectively.

The five key elements in the Greek case are capital controls, the banking system, the cash system, the Bank of Greece, and exchange-rate management. Let me take them up one by one.

Capital controls. It has often been observed that under capital controls, a euro in Cyprus is worth less than a euro elsewhere. Why is that? Because, obviously, you could buy a nominal euro's worth of deposits in a Cypriot bank for less than a euro outside. The discount was, in effect, an exchange rate. Conclusion: *capital controls are a form of exit—temporary and reversible to be sure—but nevertheless. The name on the currency hasn't changed, but in all other respects, the currency did change. It changed overnight, when controls were imposed.* This is true of bank money, and it is true of paper money subject to restrictions on removal from the country.

In the Greek case, only bank money is affected, since it is impossible to stop the departure of paper money, so paper money doesn't lose value, while bank money does. That is why conversion from bank money to paper money is profitable, and people will withdraw their sixty euros every day whether they need the cash or not. Also why it pays to eliminate euro liabilities, including taxes, with bank money. Also why increasingly businesses do not accept electronic payments, preferring to insist on cash. *Bank money has already depreciated.*

The banking system. Contrary to common comment, the Greek banks are not closed yet. It remains possible to use them electronically, 24/7. It is only that *exit from the banking system* has been obstructed. You cannot pay bills outside the country except for food and medicines. You cannot remove cash from the banks except subject to the rationed limits. Otherwise, payments are being handled entirely normally—even though the unit being circulated—a bank-money "euro"—has depreciated relative to paper and to euros outside Greece.

In the event of an actual exit, nothing need change, initially. Bank-money "euros" can continue to circulate freely inside the banking system. They, however, would be withdrawn from the banking system only via paper drachma, or by transfers overseas that would be haircut to the exchange rate of the New Drachma. The value of each bank-money "euro" will therefore be *exactly, everywhere and always*, from the first minute, one New Drachma. Whatever the value of the New Drachma may be. No change in the functioning of the banking system relative to the current situation, under capital controls, is required—except that haircut on overseas transfers, which become (instantly) foreign exchange conversions. This is easily handled.

Eventually, the bank-money "euro" accounts can be converted, one for one, into New Drachma accounts. This is evidently an arduous process, but it can proceed slowly with no problem. It will be invisible to the account holder, unless it's necessary to come in sometime and sign a new signature form and get a new debit card—routine operations if spaced over time. *Contrary to our earlier thinking, there is no need for redenomination to happen simultaneously in all accounts.*

Think about it. Since bank-money "euros" are by definition each worth one ND, both can function together at the same time. And redenomination can happen over time, using whatever balance happens to be in any particular account at the moment it is converted. Funds can flow freely from ND to bank-money "euro" accounts and vice versa during the transition, using the 1:1 exchange rate. When all accounts are converted, then everyone has a new SWIFT/IBAN number with an ND code, and then capital controls affecting external purchases can, gradually, be relaxed.[1] The exchange rate eventually takes over as the controlling device.

The cash system. Cash in Greece comes from ATMs and bank teller windows. Unlike in Iraq, secure and rapid distribution channels exist. The only problem, which we never solved sensibly, is to find paper that will work quickly in the ATMs, that will be hard to counterfeit, and that will be readily accepted as money by the population. But the obvious solution has been in front of us all along: *stamped euro notes.* All that you need is a stamping machine. It could even be done by hand; the stamp doesn't need to be fancy. No one will ever counterfeit an ND by stamping a good euro note.

So where do the euro notes come from? My earlier message suggested that the ECB could just supply them, which it could, as a helpful gesture. But suppose it doesn't want to? Well then, there are —I now learn—nineteen billion euros in paper notes in the Bank of Greece. You responded that taking those would be like robbing the ECB. But actually, this is not true at all.

So long as those notes are in the Bank of Greece, they are not worth nineteen billion. They are not money until released to the banking system. What are they? Just so much fancy paper. The price of the paper and printing is all that they are worth. By converting them with a stamp to New Drachma, Greece would have done nothing material to the ECB; it can easily reimburse the printing costs.

The New Drachma, stamped from euro notes, can go directly into the ATMs, and they can be restocked overnight or perhaps on a weekend. Initial supply problem solved. And remember that with bank-money "euros" still in the banks, but paper ND the only way to reduce those balances, people will no longer have any incentive to pull their money from the banks. So nineteen billion should last a good while, until a print order can be filled for proper bank notes.

The Bank of Greece. The Bank of Greece would need to be declared bankrupt, its functions transferred to a new entity, and the E[mergency] L[liquidity] A[ssistance] treated as a liability of the bankrupt institution. This and the necessary temporary nationalization of the commercial banks would prevent the ECB from seizing bank-money "euro" deposits. But ultimately, the new banking entity buys those "euro" 1:1 with New Drachma, and returns them to the ECB as an offset to the ELA. So—as a reward for playing nice—the ECB gets the ELA treated as a super-senior liability. In return for which, it could continue to supply stamped paper euro notes to serve as ND in the transition, and it could extend a swap line.

The exchange rate. The final element is exchange-rate policy. Here capital controls will help, since they will prevent mass flight from the New Drachma. Bank nationalization will prevent the making of speculative loans in ND that could be then sold to undermine the currency—the famous "one-way bets" that Soros used against Thailand.

But the main way to stabilize the ND after a suitable depreciation —say 30 percent—*is to obtain swap lines.*[2] The ECB might be induced to provide one, as a favor in return for getting the ELA reimbursed in the preferential manner described above. Alternatives include the Federal Reserve, the Bank of England, the Swiss, or the Chinese. It would not take much, from the standpoint of any big country, to put the ND on a solid footing and give the Greek state the liquidity it requires. If adroitly handled, surely someone would do it in order to prevent someone else from doing it first.[3]

This is all for the moment academic. Some of it just restates what I have sent before. And there may be some flaw in my reasoning. But so far I haven't spotted what it is. Unless there is one, the

Greece, Europe, and the United States

The full brutality of the European position on Greece emerged last weekend, when Europe's leaders rejected the Greek surrender document of July 9 and insisted instead on *unconditional surrender plus reparations*. The new diktat—formally accepted by Greece yesterday—requires fifty billion euros' worth of "good assets"—which incidentally do not exist—to be transferred to a privatization fund; all financial legislation passed since SYRIZA took control of Parliament in January to be rolled back; and the "troika" (the European Commission, the European Central Bank, and the International Monetary Fund) to return to Athens. From now on, the Greek government must get approval from these institutions before introducing "relevant" legislation—indeed, even before opening that legislation for public comment. In short: as of now, Greece is no longer an independent state.

Comparisons have been drawn to the Treaty of Versailles, which set Europe on the path to Nazism after the end of World War I.

Harper's, July 2015

But the 1968 Soviet invasion of Czechoslovakia, which crushed a small country's brave experiment in policy independence, is almost as good an analogy. In crushing Czechoslovakia, the invasion also destroyed the Soviet Union's reputation, shattering the illusions that many sympathetic observers still harbored. It thus set the stage for the final collapse of Communism, first among the parties of western Europe and then in the USSR itself.

Six months ago one could hope that SYRIZA's electoral victory would spark a larger discussion of austerity's failure and inspire a continent-wide search for better solutions. But once it became clear that there was no support for this approach from Spain, Portugal, or Ireland; only polite sympathy from Italy and France; and implacable hostility from Germany and points north and east, the party's goal narrowed. SYRIZA's objective became carving out space for a policy change in Greece alone. Exit from the euro was not an option, and the government would not bluff. SYRIZA's only tool was an appeal to reason, to world opinion, and for help from outside. With these appeals, the Greeks argued forcefully and passionately for five months.

In this way, the leaders of the Greek government placed a moral burden on Europe. Theirs was a challenge aimed at the vision of "sustainable growth" and "social inclusion" that has been written into every European treaty from Rome to Maastricht—a challenge aimed at the soul of the European project, if it still had a soul. No one in the Greek government entertained illusions on that point; all realized that Greece might arrive at the end of June weakened, broke, and defenseless. But given the narrow margins for maneuver, which were restricted both by SYRIZA's platform and the Greek people's attachment to Europe, it was the only play they had.

European creditors responded with surprise, irritation, exasperation, obstinacy, and finally fury. At no time did the logic of the Greek argument—about the obvious failure, over the past five years, of austerity policies to produce the predicted levels of growth—make any dent. Europe did not care about Greece. After resigning as Greek finance minister, Yanis Varoufakis described the negotiation process:

> The complete lack of any democratic scruples on behalf of the supposed defenders of Europe's democracy. The quite clear understanding on the other side that we are on the same page analytically. . . . [And yet] to have very powerful figures look at you in the eye and say, "You're right in what you're saying, but we're going to crunch you anyway."

What Europe's "leaders" do care about is power. They posture for their own parliaments and domestic polities. There is an eastern bloc, led by Finland, which is right-wing and ultra–hard line. There is a model-prisoner group—Spain, Ireland, and Portugal—which is faced with Podemos and Sinn Fein at home and cannot admit that austerity hasn't worked. There is a soft pair, France and Italy, which would like to dampen the threats from Marine Le Pen and Beppe Grillo. And there is Germany, which, it is now clear, *cannot* accept debt relief inside the Eurozone, because such relief would allow other countries in trouble to make similar demands. Europe's largest creditor would then face a colossal write-off, and the Germans would face the stunning realization that the vast debts built up to finance their exports over the past fifteen years will never be repaid.

SYRIZA was not some Greek fluke; it was a direct consequence of European policy failure. A coalition of ex-Communists, unionists, Greens, and college professors does not rise to power anywhere except in desperate times. That SYRIZA did rise, overshadowing the Greek Nazis in the Golden Dawn Party, was, in its way, a democratic miracle. SYRIZA's destruction will now lead to a reassessment, everywhere on the continent, of the "European project." A progressive Europe—the Europe of sustainable growth and social cohesion—would be one thing. The gridlocked, reactionary, petty, and vicious Europe that actually exists is another. It cannot and should not last for very long.

What will become of Europe? Clearly the hopes of the pro-European, reformist left are now over. That will leave the future in the hands of the anti-European parties, including UKIP, the National Front in France, and Golden Dawn in Greece. These are ugly, racist, xenophobic groups; Golden Dawn has proposed in its platform concentration camps for immigrants. The only counter, now, is for progressive and democratic forces to regroup behind the banner of *national* democratic restoration. Which means that the Left in Europe must also now swing against the euro.

As that happens, should the United States continue to support the euro, aligning ourselves with failed policies and crushed democratic protests? Or should we let it be known that we are indifferent about which countries are in or out? Surely the latter represents the sensible choice. After all, Poland, the Czech Republic, Croatia, and Romania (not to mention Denmark and Sweden, or for that matter the UK) are still out, and they will probably remain so—no one thinks they will fail or drift to Putin because of that.

So why should the euro—plainly now a fading dream—be propped up? Why shouldn't getting out be an option? Independent technical, financial, and moral support for democratic allies seeking exit would, in these conditions, help to stabilize an otherwise dangerous and destructive mood.

Plan B

I have known Paul Krugman for forty years. We spar occasionally, but on most issues we are allies and we are personal friends. I admire him, and trust his discretion. And he knows where I've been—admittedly, on and off—for the past five months.

So how can he write something like this, without sending me an email to check?

> Tsipras apparently allowed himself to be convinced, some time ago, that euro exit was completely impossible. It appears that Syriza didn't even do any contingency planning for a parallel currency (I hope to find out that this is wrong).

> Two errors in two sentences. How do I know? I was Plan B.

Previously unpublished, July 2015. Yanis discouraged me from publishing this, for two reasons: the volatile political situation surrounding the collapse of the negotiations and the government's capitulation, and his feeling that the text was a bit self-serving. He was right on both points; I include the piece here as a short summary of the major issues that faced the Plan B team.

In an interview published Monday in the *New Statesman*, former Greek Finance Minister Yanis Varoufakis revealed the existence of a "war cabinet" in the ministry:

> We had a small group, a "war cabinet" within the ministry, of about five people that were doing this: so we worked out in theory, on paper, everything that had to be done [to prepare for/in the event of a Grexit]. But it's one thing to do that at the level of 4–5 people, it's quite another to prepare the country for it. To prepare the country an executive decision had to be taken, and that decision was never taken.

To be precise, the "war cabinet" came into existence around mid-March, more or less at a meeting in London. We never called it that, referring to ourselves as the Plan B (or Plan X) team. We continued in function until early May, at which time we presented a long summary memorandum to the finance minister. The memo outlined the major steps, legal authorities and issues, and operational problems likely to be associated with leaving the Eurozone—a process for which no clear path or close precedent exists.

We worked in absolute secrecy, using secure communications and often operating off-site or from out of the country. On one occasion when we briefed the minister (in Paris), cell phones were placed in a hotel fridge. Even our existence could, if it had become known, have exposed Yanis Varoufakis to even more harsh public attack (he was getting plenty), which could have cost him his job and destroyed the Brussels negotiations. Worse, it could have triggered the bank panic that we all feared, triggering exit and leaving us exposed to blame for causing the collapse of the euro. (In late June, precisely by raising the specter of exit through a paper issued by the Bank of Greece, the ECB helped to provoke a late rush from the banks, which rationalized capital controls.) Our security was never breached—and now we have to face the consequence, to be criticized for, supposedly, not existing.

To develop our ideas, we relied on published literature (of which there was not much), comparative experiences especially in South America, some very discreet soundings around Athens, and our own economic and financial knowledge and common sense.

Among the questions we took up were the issues of capital controls, scrip or parallel currency, and outright exit from the Eurozone. Among the difficulties we discussed were the fact that Greece has thousands of ports of entry and exit—every boat dock in the country; the question of how scrip would be distributed and to whom, whether electronically or on paper; the problem of getting banknotes printed; the question of how long stocks of fuel would last; security for shops and supermarkets; and whether the pharmaceutical companies needed to be paid. We thought about how the pensions work, how the ATMs are used, whether you could really explain IOUs to the Greek people, and whether you could issue IOUs and then, eventually, *not* leave the euro. I believe we covered the major issues, from treaty provisions to emergency powers to bank recapitalization to critical supplies and services, reasonably well.

By early May, we had done what we could. The next step would have been to convene working groups throughout the Greek government, so that ideas could be tested against local knowledge and teams would be ready when needed. For that, the authority of the prime minister was required. And there was a certainty that once this was given, information would start to leak. To begin with, there was the basic fact that the Bank of Greece is not a state entity but a private corporation, controlled by an appointee of the previous government and by the European Central Bank. Any leak in their direction would have opened the entire process to direct knowledge of officials in Frankfurt, who might have reacted—since exit implies default, including to the ECB—by pulling the emergency liquidity assistance that underpinned the Greek banking system. No briefing of the prime minister happened, no decision to proceed to the next steps ever came, and that, as they say, was that.

Our job was not to advocate for the course of action—only to prepare, and that alone biased us toward caution. Listing all the problems made the process seem long, arduous, painful, and deeply threatening to social welfare and the survival of the state. We worried about the capacity of the Greek administration to handle the many tasks and about the ability of the Greek people to bear up. Still, I'm now convinced that we got this key political question—whether an exit would be too hard to handle—quite wrong. I now think that the process could be made—not easy, but manageable—and that it will be, some day, in Greece or somewhere else. But that is a story for another time.

THIRTY-ONE

Statement on the Ministry of Finance Working Group

I spent five months, from early February through early July, in close association with the Greek finance minister, Yanis Varoufakis, and was part of the working group that did contingency planning for potential attempts to asphyxiate the Greek government, including aggressive moves to force the country out of the euro. Since a great deal of public confusion has now arisen over this effort, the following should be stated.

(1) At no time was the working group engaged in advocating exit or any policy choice. The job was strictly to study the operational issues that would arise if Greece were forced to issue scrip or if it were forced out of the euro.

Yanis Varoufakis blog, July 2015. I made this statement in order to quell an ugly movement to scapegoat Yanis for the collapse of the Greek position. Along with other revelations, and especially the strong defense given to Yanis in Parliament by Alexis Tsipras, it largely succeeded.

(2) The group operated under the axiom that the government was fully committed to negotiating within the euro, and took extreme precautions not to jeopardize that commitment by allowing any hint of our work to reach the outside world. There were no leaks whatever, until the existence of the group was disclosed by the former finance minister himself, in response to criticism that his ministry had made no contingency plans when it was known that forces within the Eurozone were planning the forced exit of Greece.

(3) The existence of preliminary plans could not play any role in the Greek negotiating position, since their circulation (before there was a need to implement them) would have destabilized government policy.

(4) Apart from one late, inconclusive telephone conversation between MP Costas Lapavitsas and myself, we had no coordination with the Left Platform, and our working group's ideas had little in common with theirs.

(5) Our work ended for practical purposes in early May, with a long memorandum outlining major issues and scenaria that we studied.

(6) My work in this area was unpaid and unofficial, based on my friendship with Yanis Varoufakis and on my respect for the cause of the Greek people.

THIRTY-TWO

A Note to the Editors at the Guardian

I wonder if you consider it normal practice to name people as potential criminal defendants—thereby giving worldwide credence to the allegations—without checking, at all, into the plausibility of the claims?

Your story suggests that I headed a group that "allegedly hacked taxpayers' accounts," that I was part of a "criminal gang," and that I might face charges of "participating in a criminal organization."[1]

A little bit of checking would have helped to establish that (a) I have no relevant computer skills; (b) no knowledge of the Greek language; (c) was not present in Athens between March 20 and

Correspondence, July 2015. In response, the *Guardian*'s editor conceded that it would have been better had they contacted me for a comment. They later added my rebuttal to their original article, obscuring the fact that they had failed to seek a comment in the first place. For my part, my criticism here of the reporter was off base; it was the editors who were at fault. As a general matter, the role of the *Guardian* and the *Financial Times* as the mouthpieces of the Brussels apparat, throughout the Greek drama, is one for which I cordially hope their editors fry in hell.

June 4, during which time the actual working group, with which I was involved, did its actual work; (d) have never accessed, or even touched, a finance ministry computer.

One way that your reporter, Helena Smith, might have checked, would have been to send a simple message in my direction, asking for comment. I'm not hard to find.

Your reporter also made no effort to identify the "private citizens" allegedly behind the allegations, or to explore either their evidence or their motives. Instead, she cites as one of her authorities an opposition MP, without mentioning that the opposition just suffered a devastating political defeat, from which it is (fairly obviously) casting about for ways to recoup.

A bit of thought on the point could, possibly, have led her to take a slightly skeptical view of the allegations, and to perhaps wonder whether they had any plausible basis in fact.

As noted above, this is an off-the-record message. I'm not especially interested in a right of reply; other media outlets have given me that chance. I would be gratified to see a further article in the *Guardian* that is based on a bit of actual reporting, both with respect to myself and with respect to Yanis Varoufakis, against whom the charges made are equally baseless, and even more political.

Death Spiral Ahead?

The Greek Parliament has now voted to surrender control of the Greek state to platoons of bureaucrats from Brussels, Frankfurt, and Berlin, who will now reimpose the full policy regime against which Greeks rebelled in January 2015—and which they again rejected, by overwhelming majority, in the referendum of July 5.

The orders from Brussels will impose strict new rules on the Greek people in the supposed interest of paying down Greece's debt. In return, the Europeans and the IMF will put up enough new money so that they themselves can appear to be repaid on schedule—thus increasing Greece's debt—and the European Central Bank will continue to prop up the Greek banking system.

A hitch has already appeared in the plan: the International Monetary Fund, whose approval is required, has pointed out—correctly —that the Greek debt cannot be paid, and so the Fund cannot participate unless the debt is restructured. Now Germany, Greece's

Politico, July 2015

main creditor, faces a new decision: either grant debt relief, or force Greece into formal default, which would cause the ECB to collapse Greece's banks and force the Greeks out of the euro.

There are many ways to rewrite debt, and let's suppose the Germans find one they can live with. The question arises: What then?

An end to the immediate crisis is likely to have some good near-term effect. The Greek banks will "reopen," probably on Monday, and the European Central Bank will raise the ceiling on the liquidity assistance on which they rely for survival. The ATMs will be filled, although limits on cash withdrawals and on electronic transfers out of the country will probably remain. There will be some talk of new public investment, funded by the European Union; perhaps some stalled road projects will restart.

With these measures, it is not impossible that the weeks ahead will see a small uptick of economic life, and certainly, any such will make big news. It's also possible that even without good news, Greece may limp along in stagnation, within the euro.

But if you walk through the requirements of Greece's new program, there is another possibility. That possibility is an economic death spiral—contraction leading to banking failure, banking failure leading to contraction—first in Greece and, later on, elsewhere in Europe.

Here's what that would look like:

Value-added tax rates—your basic regressive sales tax—will jump by 10 percentage points or more, to 23 percent, including for hotels and restaurants and including on the Greek islands. This will divert tourists to Turkey and elsewhere, damping Greece's largest industry. Also, it will drive small businesses even further to cash and tax evasion.

Tax revenues will rise at first, but then they will fall short of targets, both because economic activity falls and evasion rises. As this happens, the new program requires that public spending be cut automatically. Since most public spending goes for pensions and wages, this means that pensions and wages will be cut. Since pensioners and civil servants live on these payments, they will cut their spending—and tax revenues will fall further.

In the labor market, extreme deregulation will proceed. Collective bargaining will be suppressed; wages will therefore fall. As a result, wage labor will go off the books, into cash, even more than it already has, and pension contributions will decline again. The resulting tax losses will feed back into pension cuts.

Privatization will work through a required new fund that will, supposedly, hold fifty billion euros in Greek assets to be sold off (notwithstanding the difficulty that, according to the economy minister, public assets on that scale do not exist). Anyhow, the state electricity company will be sold, and electric rates will rise.

As all this happens, even more people will default on their mortgages. The judicial code will be rewritten to facilitate mass foreclosures, so far held in abeyance. The nonperforming loans of the banking system will then go from disastrous to catastrophic.

Now then, under these conditions, what do you think will happen to the banks?

It is possible that a surge of "confidence" will now bring cash deposits back to the banks, new interbank loans from northern Europe, new lending to small businesses, new jobs and economic growth. Possible, but not likely.

Much more likely, with every increase of the ceiling on emergency liquidity assistance (ELA), and every relaxation of capital controls, people in Greece will line up to pull cash from the banking system. They will do this because they have to, in order to live. They will do this because cash avoids taxes. They will do it because any fool can see that the banks are doomed. So deposits will go down, the ELA will go up, still more loans will go bad, and the banks will continue as zombies until—at some point—the European

Central Bank gives up and closes them down, this time for good. Greek depositors will then lose what little remains.

Meanwhile, let's return to the legal status of the new economic program. It is true that the Greek Parliament has approved it—as the prime minister said, with a "knife to the neck." But it is a point of law that a contract signed under duress is not enforceable. This point will be heard soon, and clearly, in Greek politics if not in the courts.

It will resonate, also, through Greek society. The free consent of the governed is a right, which the Greek people have now been denied. They will not take it lightly; one can expect both passive and active resistance. Street conflict—not good for tourism—will become, once again, routine. As this happens, the drachma will become a symbol of national freedom.

Eventually, the Greek majority—the 62 percent who voted "no" on July 5—will be heard from again. A government elected by that majority will not go back to negotiations. Instead, it will repeal the program, default on the debt, take the consequences, and leave the euro.[1]

So within a few months or years, what has just happened will be overturned and repudiated. And if the Greek banks have not failed yet, they will then. At that point, Greece will be poorer than it is, even now—but it will again be independent.

But wait. The death spiral dynamic isn't necessarily limited to Greece. It could start to happen in Spain, Portugal, Ireland, and perhaps Italy—beginning, as it did in Greece, with a fall-off in interbank loans from northern Europe. Bankers, it turns out, are often the first to start a run on other banks.

What the Greek government tried to do, for five months, was to forestall this dynamic, and to bring a glimmer of economic coherence—and the potential for economic survival—to the Eurozone. It tried to get its "partners" to recognize that economic policies that had failed to produce predicted recovery for five years should be reconsidered and changed. For this heresy, Greece was crucified, to set an example. And an example it will become.

But the lesson the good citizens of the other crisis countries will draw may not be what their financial masters suppose. It may be, above all, get to cash, as quickly as possible. And get out of the euro as soon as you can.

The Future of Europe

On June 8, I had the honor of accompanying the Greek finance minister, Yanis Varoufakis, to a private meeting in Berlin with the German finance minister, Wolfgang Schäuble. The meeting began with good-humored gesture, as Herr Schäuble presented to his colleague a handful of chocolate euros, "for your nerves." Yanis shared these around, and two weeks later I had a second honor, which was to give my coin to a third (ex-)finance minister, Professor Giuseppe Guarino, dean of European constitutional scholars and the author of a striking small book on the European treaties and the euro.[1]

Professor Guarino's thesis is the following:

On 1st January 1999 a coup d'état was carried out against the EU member states, their citizens, and the European Union itself. The "coup" was not exercised by force but by cunning fraud . . . by means of Regulation 1466/97. . . . The role as-

Süddeutsche Zeitung and *American Prospect*, August 2015

signed to the growth objective by the Treaty (Articles 102A, 103 and 104c), to be obtained by the political activity of the member states . . . is eliminated and replaced by an outcome, namely budgetary balance in the medium term.

As a direct consequence: "The democratic institutions envisaged by the constitutional order of each country no longer serve any purpose. Political parties can exert no influence whatever. Strikes and lockouts have no effect. Violent demonstrations cause additional damage but leave the predetermined policy directives unscathed."

These words were written in 2013. Can there be any doubt, today, of their accuracy and of their exact application to the Greek case?

It is true that Greek governments in power before 2010 governed badly, entered into the euro under false premises, and then misrepresented Greece's deficit and debt. No one disputes this. But consider that when austerity came, the IMF and the European creditors imposed on Greece a program dictated by the doctrines of budget balance and debt reduction, including (a) deep cuts in public sector jobs and wages; (b) a large reduction in pensions; (c) a reduction in the minimum wage and the elimination of basic labor rights; (d) large regressive tax increases; and (e) fire-sale privatization of state assets.

The connection of this program to growth and recovery in Greece was wholly fraudulent. Overruling internal doubts, the IMF issued a forecast that the program would cost Greece a recession of just 5 percent of GDP, lasting one or two years, with full recovery by 2012. In fact, the Greek economy collapsed under the strain; there was a decline of more than 25 percent and no recovery for five years. Thus Greece has lost more than a full year's worth of annual output and has seen the near destruction of its major social institutions. It was in debt deflation, not recovery, at the end of 2014.

The failure of the creditors' program destroyed three prime ministers in Greece: George Papandreou, Lucas Papademos, and Antonio Samaras. It also destroyed the entire political order, dominated until then by New Democracy and PASOK. And so in January 2015 the Greek people elected a new government, built on a left-right coalition between two parties that had never before seen power, SYRIZA and AN-EL, linked only by shared commitment to changed policies for Greece, inside the euro and inside Europe.

The new government did not ask for new financial aid. The government always understood that the country would have to live within its means going forward. It accepted major elements of the previous program, with respect to taxes and public administration. What it requested, primarily, was respect for labor rights as guaranteed in all other European countries, protection of low-income pensioners, reasonable management of privatization, and relief from destructive austerity and unpayable debts.

What was the response? The European creditors and the IMF met the Greek proposals with hostility, obstruction, and refusal. The governments of Finland, the Baltic states, and Slovakia rejected them on ideological grounds. Those of Spain, Portugal, and Ireland rejected them from fear of the effect on their own politics. Italy, France, and the Commission expressed sympathy but did little. Minister Schäuble spelled out the choice: Greece could either adhere to the previous program, in full, or leave the euro and perhaps also the European Union.

From the beginning, this position was backed by threats. In late January, Eurogroup President Jeroen Dijsselbloem, visiting in Athens, threatened Greece with the destruction of its banking system. On February 4 the ECB revoked a waiver permitting Greek banks to discount government debt, and so provoked a slow run that culminated in late June; meanwhile, Greece made 3.5 billion euros in payments as a sign of good faith. When the Greek government, frustrated and broke, turned to a referendum, the creditors retaliated by closing the banks and imposing capital controls. When the Greek people stood up and said "no," the retaliation deepened, and in July the government was forced to its knees.

Since then, on three occasions and most recently on August 13, the Greek Parliament has been obliged to pass packages of legislation dictated from Brussels and Berlin. The legislation raises regressive sales taxes, while eliminating a withholding tax on capital transferred abroad. It cuts pensions—in some cases below one hundred euros per month—and sets the stage for further cuts to come. It sets the stage for ongoing cuts in the public sector, in health and education, cuts in wages, for the liquidation of many private businesses, for a wave of home foreclosures, and for the privatization at whatever price—over thirty years—of remaining public assets, including land held by the Greek government. It removes key areas of public responsibility, including economic and budget statistics and tax collection, from Greek hands and places them under the authority of the creditors. Going into the structure of the Greek economy in minute detail, the list of imposed changes is very long.

The European treaties hold that the European Union is founded on the principle of representative democracy; there is even a "principle of proximity," which holds that decisions should be taken by governmental levels as close as possible to those being affected. But within the Eurozone, this is now inverted. Greece is a colony; its fractious citizens have been dispossessed, and the place will be "modernized" against their will. Those who cannot bear it will have no choice but to leave, or again to rebel; those who do neither will probably sink back into the deep psychological depression that prevailed before the rise of SYRIZA briefly suffused the country with hope.

For progressive forces elsewhere in Europe, and especially for the young, these facts pose a difficult challenge. The hope for negotiated change within the euro has been tested, with brutal results. The fact of technocratic dictatorship within the euro is plain to everybody. Voters in the next country to rebel against the stranglehold of Eurozone policies will take note. That Greece was forced to explore the means of exit will also bear on future experience, as with improved knowledge and contingency planning—planning that will now become habitual and more or less open for every opposition movement faced with the possibility of power—the cost of making that transition, seemingly prohibitive to the Greeks this past spring, will decline.

Immediately, the Greek defeat has weakened the rising force in the next country to face elections, namely the anti-austerity, pro-European upstart party Podemos in Spain. But the effect in Ireland, which is less wedded to the euro, could be different; Ireland trades with the UK and the United States and does not have the same emotional links to Europe as Spain or Greece. And then the scene will shift to Italy, still in recession and political flux, and to France, which already has a powerful antieuro party on the right, the National Front of Marine Le Pen.

These political consequences will keep the euro under strain, deepened by the ongoing failure of the neoliberal economic regime. It therefore seems likely that the euro will, at some point, in some country, crack. The decision to initiate a breakup could come from the left or the right. In any case such a decision will destroy, as events in Greece have destroyed, the previous political structures. A breakup, if it goes badly, could make things worse. What will happen to the European Union after that is anyone's guess.

Professor Guarino's proposal is to try to save Europe—that is, the European Union—by repealing the illegitimate regulations that now strangle it. It is to refound the Union on the letter and spirit of the treaties that were usurped in 1999. Those treaties firmly assert the priority of economic growth and the principle of democratic sovereignty—equally applied to countries in or out of the euro. Those are principles that have no practical application inside the Eurozone today.

Can the euro be reformed? The Greek case will convince many that it cannot. And if the alternative is disorderly and uncontrolled exits, precipitated by countries in extreme straits and political upheaval, then it might be wise to prepare some new system, one that might, at the right moment, replace the euro with a more flexible, but still managed, multicurrency scheme. This is not an outlandish thought—after all, the gold standard that collapsed in 1933 was replaced in 1944 by just such a system, devised at Bretton Woods.

The trick is to get the job done without the intervening chaos.

THIRTY-FIVE

What the Greek Memorandum Means

WITH DANIEL MUNEVAR

It is a lie from the first line: "Greece has requested support from its European partners . . ." Thus begins the "Memorandum of Understanding for a three-year ESM programme," which sets the conditions with which Greece must comply, in order to avoid being ruled in default on its debts.

The reality is that the Greek prime minister, Alexis Tsipras, was bludgeoned into accepting the terms that follow in this long and depressing document, under threat that the banking system of his country, entirely controlled by the European Central Bank, would otherwise be demolished, and that he would be forced to manage a disorderly exit from the euro, for which his government did not feel—and for which in fact it wasn't—decently prepared.

For what purpose, this supposed support? The document continues: "to restore sustainable growth, create jobs, reduce inequali-

Dissent, August 2015

ties, and to address the risks to its own financial stability and to that of the euro area." Let us take these up in turn.

"*Restore* sustainable growth." In reality Greece has not enjoyed sustainable growth under the euro, which is to say, not since 1999 at least. Growth in the entire period before 2010 was built on unsustainable debt, followed since then by deep and ongoing decline.

"Create jobs." Here the record of the previous memorandums, in force since 2010 and highly similar to the present one, is not reassuring. Under their guidance, Greek unemployment has reached 29 percent overall and around 60 percent for the young, with no sign of improvement so far.

"Reduce inequalities." The cynicism is to weep. The memorandum sharply increases taxes on the poor, reduces them in several respects on the rich, and cuts pensions at the very bottom of the scale. Meanwhile farmers and dairies and small professionals such as pharmacists will be swept away by northern European agribusiness and chain stores.

As for risks to financial stability, there are two. The first is the state of the Greek economy, in which some two-fifths of bank loans are nonperforming. The memorandum does nothing about these loans, except to establish a creditor-controlled "liquidator" for Greek businesses and homeowners. As the economy gets worse, of course the liquidations will increase.

The second risk arose from the actions of the ECB since January, when the new Greek government came in. In violation of its charter, which is to promote financial stability, the ECB responded by prompting a run on Greek banks, in anticipation of confiscation of deposits. To undo this damage, depositors are now being told that all Greek bank deposits will be covered by insurance. This would be reassuring—except that what will happen when Greece falls out of compliance with the memorandum remains unclear.

The second paragraph continues: "Success requires ownership of the reform agenda programme by the Greek authorities." But then: "the government commits to consult and agree [with the creditors] on all actions relevant [to the MoU] before these are finalized and legally adopted." Moreover, compliance with terms will be reviewed, not every year, but every quarter—twelve times over three years. Ownership is where, exactly?

Next, "The recovery strategy takes into account the need for social justice and fairness . . ." In this paragraph, the memorandum promises to attack tax evasion and "rent-seeking" while providing fifty thousand new jobs, universal health insurance, and a guaranteed minimum income. Terrific, except that tax evasion and rent-seeking are presented as the small-scale activity of petty players—not the oligarchs who specialize in both—while not a single new euro is provided for any social goal. Apparently the new jobs, health care, and guaranteed income are to be financed by cutting somewhere else in the Greek budget. Where, exactly, the document does not say.

Following this pabulum, the memorandum sets out the four pillars of policy for "sustainable recovery." These are said to be "restoring fiscal sustainability," "safeguarding financial stability," promoting "growth, competitiveness and investment," and establishing "a modern State and public administration." Of the four, a glance reveals that only one—the first—has macroeconomic content, and that is the declared target of a "primary surplus" of 3.5 percent of GDP. This fantasy goal is to be achieved, in the main, by raising the value-added tax, cutting pensions, and enforcing tax collections more sternly. It is the opposite, in short, of a sustainable recovery strategy.

The other three "pillars" consist of the following major features: (a) forced bankruptcies and foreclosures; (b) "labor market reforms" obscurely described as EU "best practice" (and specified, later in the document, to be decided by the creditors themselves), plus "ambitious privatization"; and (c) "independence" of the tax administration and of the statistical services, which again means that the creditors and not the Greek state will be in control.

"Success will require the sustained implementation of agreed policies over many years." Never mind that there is no agreement here, only dictation. This statement, which begins the fifth major paragraph, concedes that there is no standard for success. Continued actual stagnation and failure in Greece will be passed off as either unsustained effort or insufficient passage of time. This means that long-term private investment in the local Greek economy is discouraged from the start, since failure to meet the targets will trigger further tax increases and cuts in demand.

Skipping ahead a bit, one gets to some of the ugly details. As "prior actions," to be enacted by Parliament before funds are disbursed, the Greek government is required to raise taxes specifically on farmers; raise the tonnage tax on shipping (which will, as Yanis Varoufakis observes, persuade the shipowners to move their base to Cyprus); cut subsidies for heating oil in half; and (as if by magic) cure the ills of Greek tax collection. The latter will be tricky, given that income taxes on farmers and on rents are magnets for increased tax evasion. In addition, "the authorities commit to legislate in October 2015 credible structural measures" to raise another 1 percent of GDP in taxes by 2018. If the courts rule against any measure, the government will "take offsetting measures as needed to meet the fiscal targets." Nothing in the Greek constitution, in other words, can stand in the way.

Long sections of the memorandum deal with pensions and health care. Pensions must be cut by 1 percent of GDP by 2016. Mandatory contributions to fund health care will rise. Access to the "basic, guaranteed contributory, and means-tested pensions" will come "only at the attainment of the statutory normal retirement age of 67" (raised from 60 for women and 65 for men over the course of the past two bailout deals). By 2019, the "solidarity grant" to the lowest-income pensioners, known as EKAS, will end. Meanwhile, the government will again start collecting fees in hospital surgeries from the poor, and will take measures that target the remaining Greek pharmaceutical companies in ways that will favor multinational producers—ignoring the fact that Greek consumers today benefit from some of the lowest drug prices in Europe.

On privatization, the memorandum sets out a long list, from gas and electricity and water to transport and public assets, including airports and ports. The document specifies that they will be sold or auctioned or in some other way opened to private businesses, who will (as a general rule) raise fees and defer maintenance, since there is no other way to make money in a collapsing country. Here is specified the absurd fifty billion euro asset fund—a target so high that it has the practical effect of assuring that every euro actually earned from fire sales will be paid to creditors or used for bank recapitalization, with nothing for growth or investment.

What does Greece get for this? Some eighty-six billion euros will flow in—and right back out again, to be recorded as payments on the debt and bank recapitalization. So Greece gets, for now, to stay supposedly current, as new debt replaces the old debt coming due. And yet the memorandum says nothing about restructuring or debt relief, nothing about the sustainability of the debt in the long run. That will be decided and judged, we hear, in October, when the IMF will decide to join the program, or—more likely—to walk away.

Yanis Varoufakis has annotated the memorandum in full detail, and it is not our purpose here to duplicate his work. Rather, let us consider the larger implications of this document.

In Greece the prospect is for the liquidation of everything. As taxes rise and purchasing power falls, it would take an act of God to keep most businesses afloat or homeowners in their homes once the tourist season ebbs and the weather grows cold. A double death spiral will probably follow: on one side, tax revenues will ebb, bringing on further cuts in pensions and public payrolls; on the other, more businesses and homeowners will default on their loans, deepening the troubles of the banking system. The economy, or what remains of it, will go toward cash and barter, with multinationals moving in on utilities, ports, airports, hotels, and other cash-cow operations. Ultimately, the ECB will be forced at some point to shut the banks—and no doubt reopen them, if deposits remain guaranteed, under foreign control. Otherwise, in the ultimate liquidation, the deposits will simply disappear.

Political consequences are already in motion. The old governing parties, which brought on the disaster, will continue to implode. But now SYRIZA, which rose on a wave of rebellion and hope, has also split, with a new antieuro politics taking over on the left, as it has on the extreme right. These two forces will contest, for a while, over the disaffected and destroyed population. If the new Popular Unity party wins the confidence of the 61 percent who voted "no" in the July referendum, then the September snap election would take Greece out of the memorandum and out of the euro. But this is unlikely; Greeks remain (in spite of everything) attached to the euro, and the snap election was called to deny a new opposition time to gel. More likely, before new political space opens in Greece, the full consequences of the memorandum will first have to be felt.

Europe is another matter. For Europeans, the Greek memorandum now stands as a symbol of what Europe has become, and the prospects for reform at the European level now seem very bleak. Spain's Podemos—which offered a SYRIZA-like model of antiausterity within the euro—has lost support following SYRIZA's defeat. In countries with elections coming later—Portugal, Ireland, France—the political consequences will continue to unfold, but it seems likely that

Back to Square Zero

The political aftermath of the Greek referendum and capitulation was entirely predictable—until suddenly it wasn't. SYRIZA split, as twenty-three deputies from the Left Platform quit the party to form Popular Unity, a new antimemorandum party openly favorable to return to the drachma. Rather than face a vote of confidence—which he would have lost, forcing an election—Alexis Tsipras resigned the prime ministership. After a brief ritual in which the other parties tried but failed to form a government, the election of September 20, 2015, was duly called.

Initial public reaction hit Tsipras hard. In the polls SYRIZA dropped to near-parity with New Democracy, and Popular Unity rose to 10 percent. But then the tide turned.

The tide turned for two major reasons. First, Tsipras was able to recast the election into a choice of personnel rather than policy, tapping into the deep antipathy of many voters toward the old

Riga, Latvia, October 19, 2015

oligarchy that had been driven from power in January, 2015. The choice was therefore between a party that would implement the program with regret and one that would implement it with pleasure. Second, the Greek government's basically decent response to the refugee crisis touched a popular chord. In deep adversity, the Greek popular mood toward the thousands of Syrians washing up on Lesbos and other islands was impressively generous.

Meanwhile, Popular Unity failed to win traction and eventually faded below the 3 percent national vote threshold required to enter Parliament. Tsipras formed a new government, just like his original one, in coalition with AN-EL, but with a handpicked slate and no immediate internal dissenters. It is a government that might last for a full term if economic conditions and popular resistance don't destroy it. Euclid Tsakalotos returned to the finance ministry, this time to implement the memorandum rather than to resist it. Yanis Varoufakis, who could neither support the capitulation nor align fully with the Left opposition, returned home.

In October, the Greek Parliament passed a host of "prior measures" stipulated in the new memorandum, in order to draw on further tranches of the loan agreement and to open a path toward eventual renegotiation of the debt. The new measures are a hotchpotch of spending and pension cuts, tax increases, market openings, measures to speed up foreclosures and the bankruptcies now expected for some forty thousand Greek firms this year. The liquidation of Greek assets, public and private, and the dispossession of the Greek people from ownership in their homeland is now the policy of Europe, and the policy of the colonial government of Greece. This is what the international press continues to describe as "reforms."

Alexis Tsipras's one hope is that by extending austerity to the oligarchs, he can make it somewhat easier—and easier to bear—on ordinary Greeks. No doubt there will be measures, some of them symbolic, to that end. But the oligarchs are hard to touch; money once out of the country is hard to track, and physical assets can often be moved. Shipowners, in particular, can easily relocate to Cyprus. And there is the fact that in important respects the creditor interests and those of the oligarchs are aligned. According to Tariq Ali, writing in the *London Review of Books*, the largest tax evader in Greece is a German construction firm, Hochtief, which holds the concession for the Athens airport.[1]

Assuming that the Greek Parliament meets the requirements, discussions will open in late 2015 on the Greek debt, which will tend to highlight the policy differences between the IMF and the Europeans on that question. For the Greeks, however, it makes little immediate difference what happens to the debt; so long as they are locked into the policies of the memorandum, those policies will largely govern the economic outcomes.

In economics nothing is certain, but the most likely next phase will come into focus when the Greek economy again fails to meet its specified fiscal targets, thanks to stagnant or declining activity and faltering tax collections. This could take six months to develop; it could take a year or longer.

When the program begins to fail, the creditors will then point to flaws, real or contrived, in the execution of the program, and they will be entitled to demand still further cuts in spending and pensions. The government will then again face the choice: to capitulate and comply, or to default and abandon the euro. Perhaps one long-term benefit of our work on Plan B in the spring of 2015 will be to clarify this choice, and to demystify the dangers and the opportunities in the second course. And if not in Greece, perhaps the lessons learned there will be helpful somewhere else.

Meanwhile, the political scene in Europe is shifting in ominous ways. In Catalonia an independence party has won a regional majority, as did another in Scotland; both are antiausterity but pro-European. Yet the Greek experience is bearing against the pro-European Left in Spain, Portugal, and Ireland, as citizens of those countries assess the possibility of getting a good-faith improvement of policy within the euro. That possibility, a tenet of the program of Podemos in Spain, for example, has been clearly shown to be, for practical purposes, nonexistent.

Indeed, the Left in Europe has been given a hard double lesson by events. The first is that governments of the Left, no matter how free from corruption, no matter how pro-European, are not acceptable to the community of creditors and institutions that make up the European system. The second is that, per contra, right-wing governments can get away with policies that governments of the Left cannot. In Spain at present writing there is a recovery going on—not because the reactionary government of Mariano Rajoy has made austerity work but because it has abandoned it, with a wink and a nod—for now—from the European Commission and Central Bank.

In France, Britain, and possibly Finland, it is the anti-European Right that has so far gained ground as the reputation of the European institutions crumbles. In Britain European sentiment will be tested in a referendum. In France the test will come with the presidential elections of 2017, trending at the moment toward Marine Le Pen. In Italy, France, and Britain, Left movements are attempting to pull themselves together, to come to grips with their own prior blind devotion to the transnational project. All of this is influenced, to some degree, by the galvanizing example of the Greek revolt of 2015, as the drama of the refugees reveals just how shallow the well of European solidarity has become.

The pot stirs. The plot thickens. The edifice of European unity shudders, under the weight of thoughtless, self-serving mistreatment of a small country which, for all of its own flaws, dared for a few months to gather its courage and say "no."

A Final Word

Madrid, October 21, 2015

This has been a year of political miracles and great struggles. In January, a battered and beleaguered Greek people placed a brave bet on Alexis Tsipras, on my friend Yanis Varoufakis, and on a party of trade unionists, ecologists, and college professors that had never before held power. In September, to much consternation, the member-voters of the British Labour Party broke with the pallid politics of New Labour, placing a brave bet on Jeremy Corbyn. And day before yesterday, the voters of Canada overthrew ten years of austerity and restated their faith and confidence in the party that created Canada's welfare state, and from which my own family descends.[1]

These events build, in some cases without knowing it, on the intellectual and political upheavals that have returned democracy to South America since the 1980s and that has brought that continent,

Madrid, October 21, 2015. Adapted from my keynote speech to the Second Annual Trade Union Congress on Labor, Economy, and Society.

which was the laboratory of neoliberalism in the 1970s, a measure of prosperity and social progress. In all of these places the common bond is the rise of new economic thinking, rooted in the successful social democratic traditions of the twentieth century and enriched by harsh experience and political maturation.

In the first place, the new thinking rejects imposed doctrine; it rejects the ideas of economists from what was once a right-wing fringe, who seized control of the profession, its leading universities, and commanding dogmas a generation back. That doctrine consisted of a single line of thought—*la pensée unique*—or the "Washington consensus," which sought to impose on all countries the regime of fiscal austerity, the modern monetary equivalent of the gold standard, combined with deregulation, privatization, and the associated stripping of public assets, covered by the notion that "structural reform" would unlock the hitherto imprisoned forces of productivity growth. The failure of this doctrine was clear already in the developing world with the crises of 1997 in Asia and 1998 in Russia, and it became clear to all sensible people in Europe and in the United States in 2007 and 2008. But in Europe, especially, bad ideas are written in constitutional stone, and the struggle to change them is that of the stone mason and not that of the poet alone.

Philosophically we forsake the dogmatic for the practical and the singular for the plural—not one alternative, but many alternatives. For this reason, no sensible person replaces neoliberal rules with revolutionary rhetoric, nor even with the simple Keynesianism that would rely on "stimulus" alone. Instead a pragmatic economics must have multiple lines, working together. These include:

An investment strategy, designed locally, adapted to the conditions and opportunities and special qualities of people and place.

A human strategy, for education, training, and employment, for wages, jobs, and equality.

An insurance strategy, to reduce social, personal, and family risks and to protect the vulnerable, so that people feel free to take economic and creative chances.

A business and financial strategy, to foster sustainable growth and to quell speculation.

An environmental strategy, to conserve resources and fight climate change.

A democratic strategy, to foster cooperative effort and to legitimate the common project, while protecting the rights of discussion and dissent.

These are the ideas that in broad terms motivated the Greek revolt. Are they utopian? On the contrary. They are built on the lived experience of the most successful development projects, in the United States from 1900 to 1970 and in Europe after the war: the Progressive Era, the New Deal, the Marshall Plan, and the postwar reconstruction that produced what the French call the *trente glorieuses*. They recognize that the true foundation of prosperity is not technology and not education, both of which can be found, or moved, anywhere. Nor is it the concrete of highway projects and hydroelectric dams. It is, rather, the system of social purpose achieved by checks and balances, by effective and autonomous and reasonable regulation, by the dynamic equilibrium of private profit and public purpose, of the individual and the collective, of the firm, the trade union, and the state.

The great economists from Adam Smith to John Maynard Keynes understood this. "Institutionalism" and "structuralism" are the proper formal names for the economic tradition; "pragmatism" is what we call the philosophical school, "progressivism" is its political manifestation, and "yes, we can" is its expression in the popular will.[2] In that spirit, let us continue.

Appendix

A Summary of Plan X

The most sensitive task I undertook for the finance ministry was to coordinate the work of a small group that prepared a contingency plan for the possibility that negotiations would fail and that Greece would be forced to exit the Eurozone. The plan took the form of a memorandum, initially submitted at the start of May, and finally updated in late June. We stressed, always, that exit from the euro would be complicated, disruptive, and risky; it was a step to take only when all efforts to remain in the Eurozone under acceptable conditions had failed. This appendix outlines some of the major technical questions that concerned us. Some of the key procedures discussed are, in my current view, not the correct way to proceed. I have added a few footnotes on those points.

We divided the key areas that the Greek government would face into the following broad categories: 1) legal issues, including the governing statutes, assets, and exposures of the Bank of Greece; 2) rapid reconstruction of the banking system, under capital controls in the new currency; 3) public debt-payment priorities and restructuring terms; 4) critical supplies and emergency management; and 5) public security. We stressed that our discussion of these issues could only be preliminary, since we had no ability to conduct an open discussion of the ways, means, and politics of the various steps; we also stressed that we did not believe the European partners would cooperate in smoothing the transition. We were therefore preparing a worst-case scenario, in which exit would have to be accomplished quickly, under stress, and without significant external support.

The Basic Scenario

The basic scenario leading to exit was assumed to be the following: 1) a breakdown in the negotiations, meaning inevitable default; 2) a decision by the ECB to cap or remove the ELA; 3) closure of the banks and confiscation of the remaining deposits. Since the Greek deposit insurance fund could cover only a small fraction of the value of existing euro accounts, this would imply either closing down the payments system altogether or replacing those accounts with a new currency, as quickly as possible.

Specific exit actions would be required as soon as the ECB revoked the ELA: (a) declaration of a state of emergency; (b) immediate nationalization of the Bank of Greece, or alternatively declaration of bankruptcy, creation of a new entity, and appointment of a commissioner to run it;[1] (c) nationalization of the commercial banks and the imposition of a bank holiday; (d) redenomination of all deposits and Greek law loans into New Drachma at an initial exchange rate of 1:1;[2] (e) printing of scrip to cover wages, pensions, and suppliers, with banknotes to follow as soon as feasible;[3] (f) imposition of capital controls and withdrawal limits; (g) strong, appropriate, and visible measures to guarantee public safety, security, and essential supplies and services; (h) communications aimed at the Greek public, world opinion, and the tourist trade, to reassure all that the disruptions would be manageable and temporary; (i) a full schedule of terms for the restructuring of the external debt.

(a) State of emergency. Under Greek law, article 44 of the Constitution gives the president the power to act, at the direction of the cabinet, under extraordinary circumstances of an urgent and unforeseeable need. In that case, parliamentary approval can be deferred.

(b) Bank of Greece. According to our legal advisers, the Washington, DC, firm of Cleary Gottlieb, "nationalization of the Bank of Greece is clearly primarily a matter of Greek national law." Doing so would, however, have

put Greece in potential breach of several provisions of the TFEU (articles 123, 130). There seemed, however, no way to avoid this conflict, since Greece had to have a central bank under government control for the period of the state of emergency.

(*c*) *Commercial banks.* ECB action to haircut collateral, which took the form of Greek government bonds held by the Greek banks, would imply that the Greek commercial banks had failed and their stockholders/bondholders would be wiped out. The banks would therefore be closed and, unless the Greek state took action to prevent it, the remaining deposits would be largely offset against the ELA. Inside the euro, the ECB would presumably recapitalize the banks externally and reopen them under foreign ownership, but with little to no compensation for Greek depositors, who would lose what they had in the banks, primarily by this point the working capital of Greek businesses. To forestall this, the banks would have to be nationalized immediately under Greek law, and recapitalized in New Drachma.

(*d*) *Deposits* could be replenished (redenominated) in New Drachma, but access to them would have to be limited under capital controls to prevent capital flight and rapid depreciation. The problem here was that conversion and redenomination would take time, during which the banks would have to remain closed and the economy could function only on the basis of existing liquidity, including euro notes in circulation and trade credit. This prospect was fairly discouraging, and so we explored ways to extend liquidity through the issuance of scrip, which could have been effective for paying suppliers and civil servants but did not solve the problems of Greek business nor especially of pensioners who are accustomed to drawing their pensions in cash from the ATMs at banks.

(*e*) With ND cash unavailable at first, scrip would have to be printed at short notice to cover wages, pensions, and supplies to the extent that euros were unavailable. Presumably, most scrip would come back to the government quickly as tax payments, so that this particular form of parallel currency would be relatively short-lived, as was the case in Argentina and in various historical experiences in the United States.

(*f*) *Capital controls.* Capital controls were introduced in Greece near the end of June, under conditions similar to those we recommended, including withdrawal limits at ATMs, a blanket prohibition on payments outside the country (except for food and drug purchases authorized by the finance ministry), and no border controls on taking cash out of the country, which we did not expect to be a problem and which could not, in any event, have been enforced. The major difference between our scenario and what actually happened was that under a transition to a new currency there would be a full depreciation of both bank deposits and cash, and under those circumstances, we expected money held outside Greece to flow back into the country to take advantage of lower asset prices.

(g) Public safety, security, and supplies. We took very seriously the problems of emergency management and public order; in the event of a transition these would be major responsibilities of the defense and interior ministries. Further, it would be necessary to control and economize fuel supplies, especially for public and maritime transport, and to try to ensure uninterrupted supplies of basic medicines and of food. In general we believed that these problems could be managed, with some difficulties, especially in summer when food supplies and heating oil were not major problems.

(h) Communications. Telecommunications companies, including Vodafone, Wind, OTE, and the TV and radio stations and other local and foreign-owned MNCs providing key infrastructure would have to be put on notice to maintain services during the transition.

Further communications steps would include to notify key European partners, the institutions, the IMF, the White House, and the Federal Reserve, and to make the case for the forced necessity of the steps being undertaken. There would then follow a prime minister's speech, announcing a bank holiday and the coming conversion.

(i) Debt structure and restructuring priorities. Term sheets for restructuring of different liabilities would have to be prepared. The main goal of this exercise would be an *easily* manageable debt burden—for the absolute quantum of debt as a percentage of a conservative GDP projection and the maturity profile, as well as the minimum number of defaults. This would mean restructuring of the largest and most immediate maturities in favor of retaining smaller, longer-maturity obligations current. It should be stressed that before exit Greece had been under a currency swap line between the Federal Reserve and the ECB; continuity of US policy toward Greece therefore implies a now-separate swap line from the Federal

Reserve to the Greek central bank. I made this point many times, including in conversations with staff at the Federal Reserve; the objective was to keep lines of communication open and the response was generally understanding. But there could of course be no assurance whatever that the US government, or any other, would ride to the rescue in a crisis.

The Legal Basis for an Exit

The legal basis for exiting the euro while remaining in the European Union was never entirely clarified and remains to this day open to dispute. Based on the advice we received, we argued that the government of Greece should maintain its commitment to remain a member of the European Union, and within all other treaties to which the Greek state is party, and this point should be emphasized in all public and private statements from the outset. Emergency violations of EU treaties would then be described as temporary and to be remedied as soon as the emergency is mastered.

In our view, there was (and is) no provision that requires Greece to exit the European Union on leaving the Eurozone, and no means to expel it. While the treaties binding Greece to the euro have described that link as "irrevocable," evidently there is no firm legal meaning to that word; wills are "irrevocable" until they are revoked. But on the other hand, we could not guarantee that the European courts would agree with this interpretation; in the end, we felt, what would ultimately happen would depend largely not on the terms of the treaties but on political judgments to be made as the crisis unfolded.

On decision to exit, as an immediate step, the government would have to take control of the Bank of Greece, via presidential decree or extraordinary general meeting, as appropriate. We received information that the statutes of the Bank of Greece may require amendment to permit the introduction of a new currency, in which case the statutes would have to be amended via an extraordinary general meeting, which would have to be called immediately. We were also concerned about gold reserves—another topic on which we had no access to direct information. Securing reserves held outside Greece and assuring that they not be used to offset Bank of Greece obligations would be an important preemptive step.[4]

Under EU law, article 59 of the treaty permits capital controls to be introduced for six months, if approved by the EC and ECB. It is not clear, however, whether the ECB is required to approve capital controls in a different currency.

For private-sector debtors, as a starting point, Greece could declare both Greek law and foreign debts redenominated into New Drachma. With respect to foreign-law debts, foreign courts and counterparties will probably not accept the declaration, but the issue can be resolved by later negotiations, including between private parties.

If any wage contract provisions linking nominal wages to the price level remain in force at this date, we argued that they should be suspended indefinitely as an emergency measure and banned by law in new contracts. This is essential to prevent a wage/exchange-rate spiral leading possibly to hyperinflation in the new currency.

As noted above, Greek banks would be bankrupted by the transition; they would have to be nationalized and recapitalized with GGBs[5] in ND, preferably according to a prepared structure of equity, preferred shares, and subordinated debt. The new GGBs would have supersenior status. Deposit insurance should be announced to cover ND accounts at an acceptable level, say 100,000 ND.

The government should immediately issue tax-anticipation notes, denominated in ND. This scrip will be acceptable as taxes and exchangeable against ND notes when they become available; meanwhile, it will circulate as an alternative means of payment. TANs should be acceptable in payment of taxes at 1:1 against the euro.

On the first night, teams should meet with the banks to determine the legal status of their debts, derivatives, and financing arrangements, and to review contingency plans they may have made.

An order would have to be placed for ND notes immediately following the announcement. A full stock of ND notes would require some months to arrive and be introduced, depending on how many presses can be hired for the purpose or whether the cooperation of friendly foreign countries can be secured. The question whether any friendly large country might lend its printing presses to get new notes in circulation quickly was one we considered; it seemed a reasonable proposition in principle. Coins, we believed, could be postponed for a later date. On the other hand, we argued that steps should be taken to make debit cards as widely available as possible and to ease adoption of wireless credit devices by small firms, and to promote the use of cell phones for payments by electronic transfers, as off-the-shelf applications for this purpose are available. Cell phones can be used to transfer balances to businesses or to individual accounts. The company that implemented this system in Kenya is Vodafone, which has a substantial presence in Greece.

On the international exchanges, with no outside support and no reserves to defend it, the ND would necessarily float and depreciate. Presumably euro coins and notes would circulate meanwhile, with euro prices adjusted to reflect the depreciation of ND, or vice versa. However, given the Gresham's Law principle that bad money drives out good, it seemed likely that ND would circulate while euro would be held as reserves; achieving a reasonably stable valuation for the ND under these conditions would require very strong fiscal and trade discipline, especially at the outset, and especially if large foreign central banks declined to help. For this reason, immediate security measures would have to be taken, using all available forces to maintain public order, to protect government buildings and property, to provide emergency assistance, and to prevent looting at stores. The potentials for hoarding, shortages, and profiteering in this situation were daunting.

Further, tourists would have to be reassured that they could come in safety and with no risk of disruption or hardship. Fuel supplies for airplanes landing in Greece and for ships must be assured throughout, as this is the lifeline of tourist income. The population should be reminded that the success of the transition depends on a calm and welcoming environment for the tourist season, and there would have to be assistance available to transient populations without resources, such as migrants. Reception areas and food stations may be needed. The population should be warned to take precautions against petty crime, as euro notes will become scarce and valuable. An emergency fund for overseas travelers and other stranded persons would be helpful; this can be administered by embassies and consulates.

Workers providing essential public services, including schools, hospitals, and police, should be called to duty as though under mobilization;

the success of a transition depends on their willingness to carry on in their jobs. The government would have to warn the civil service that corruption of any type, especially extracting euro bribes from the population, will not be tolerated. Judicial personnel should be alerted to the need to investigate and prosecute reports of abuses immediately in a high-profile manner; a hot line for complaints should be set up and efficiently manned.

We argued that there should be an increase in the tax on luxuries (cars, boats, appliances, etc.), and indeed on durable goods of almost all types, to levels aimed at discouraging such purchases for the time being and stabilizing the current account. The taxes can be phased down once the ND stabilizes. We further argued that the government should consider imposing rent controls—initially, a ninety-day rent freeze—to prevent out-of-control escalation of rentals by some landlords who may face ND payments and euro liabilities.

For the case of mortgages denominated in euros and owed to entities outside Greece, redenomination may be blocked, in which case foreclosure can be followed by a right to rent with option to repurchase,[6] limiting dispossession and giving the lender incentives to come to reasonable terms with the mortgagee. Provision for a right-to-rent option can be made by legislation during the implementation phase.

Macroeconomic Policy

In the transition to a new currency, the ND will and should depreciate. For this reason a currency board arrangement is not desirable in the short run, especially since there are no hard currency assets, excepting possibly gold, to stabilize the ND; currency stabilization is not a priority use of assets that may not be available in any event. Further, establishing a currency board with support from the EU or ECB would merely reopen the discussions about conditionality.

The immediate increase in ND prices would be substantial—perhaps very substantial—and should not be predicted. To do so would merely undermine credibility, if the inflation exceeds the guidelines. Ultimately stabilizing the ND is primarily a matter of building/maintaining an effective tax system, and of controlling public expenditures; if taxes are collected in

ND, the currency will be in demand and will hold value. The government should, however, issue guidelines on profit margins in the transition and warn merchants against profiteering.

Among other points, we suggested:

Local authorities can be directed to establish boards for reviewing local behavior to ensure that businesses function normally and do not profiteer, and to encourage store credit and other accommodations to vulnerable persons.

As noted above, any remaining wage indexation to the price level should be suspended immediately and banned in new contracts by decree.

The Greek government should announce an inflation target on the order of 3–5 percent for the period *following* adjustment of the ND to a stabilized value.

We suggested, finally, that a credible international central banker may be appointed to head the new central bank of Greece.

Remaining Issues

The remaining issues covered by our memorandum were a grab bag of financial and funding questions. We were specifically and especially concerned with assuring the stability of basic supplies during a transition period, but also with the effective transition of the banking sector, with attracting foreign investment, and with the restructuring and conversion of private debts, both within Greece and between Greek debtors and creditors in other countries. We discussed, again, ways to improve tax collection by encouraging electronic payments. A final section reiterated the main timing and sequencing questions as we understood them, and reiterated that, following exit, Greece would need to maintain a small primary surplus in order to establish, and ultimately maintain, a reasonable, stable value for the new currency.

Summary

To give the reader a feel for the mood of the moment and especially my own, as these events built to a climax, I reproduce below the exact language of the conclusion to the Plan X memorandum.

A decision to exit the common currency will be a leap into the unknown. It will be an assertion of independence but also of responsibility. People's lives are at stake, as well as the survival of the elected government. The reason for doing it can only be that there is no reasonable alternative compatible with preserving democratic government in Greece. The step can be decided on only when that point has been clearly reached.

Yet there is no reason, in the end, why Greece under a national currency, free of the dogmas of the Eurozone and having adapted policy to national needs and conditions, will not be able to recover economically and eventually prove more prosperous than at present. There is a good precedent for believing that with competent management and devaluation the exit will unlock foreign and domestic investment and permit the implementation of a strategy for restored growth. Getting to that point is the challenge.

The ultimate success or failure of the transition will depend on the reaction of the Greek people, on the ability to quell dissent from opposition, far-right, external, and potentially violent sources, including provocateurs, to avoid or quell violence, and especially on the ability of the government to maintain order, to keep basic services and supplies flowing, and to establish and stabilize the new currency within a reasonable time. It will depend on the effect on the most vulnerable, and the operation will be judged, in the end, by whether a moral commitment to the Greek people was met.

Acknowledgments

This book owes everything to Yanis Varoufakis, who brought me into the Greek cause as he threw himself, heart and soul, into the struggle for his country.

Thanks to my editors on the individual pieces that make up this work: Robert Kuttner at the *American Prospect*, Michael Hirsh at *Politico*, Christopher Beha at *Harper's*, Jonathan Stein and Kenneth Murphy at *Project Syndicate*, Robert Mudge at *Deutsche Welle*, Catherine Hoffmann at the *Süddeutsche Zeitung*, and Henning Meyer at *Social Europe*. My great thanks to my agent, Wendy Strothman, and to Bill Frucht and his team at Yale University Press, who took up the manuscript with speed and skill.

In Athens I benefited from close collaboration with the most talented student to have graced the LBJ School during my career, Daniel Munevar, and from the chance to work with the dedicated staff and professionals present last spring in the Hellenic Ministry of Finance, including especially Fotini Badakima, Eleni Panaritis, and Michael Papadopoulos, as well as with talented outsiders including Glenn Kim, Brian Kim, Jeff Sachs, and a few others who might prefer not to be named. As the crisis progressed, I had valuable conversations with Giuseppe Guarino and with Michael

Marder and Elpida Hadjidaki, as well as profiting from their wonderful hospitality.

My students and my family tolerated a great deal in the spring of 2015, and as always I am deeply, deeply indebted to Ying.

Finally, I thank the brave people of Greece, who deserved a better ending.

Notes

ONE
Welcome to the Poisoned Chalice

1. The work of Heiner Flassbeck most effectively illustrates the chronic trade and financial imbalance between Germany and its trading at the heart of the European crisis.

2. Or in Ireland, where newspapers on September 12, 2015, revealed that in 2010 Jean-Claude Trichet, then president of the European Central Bank, threatened that "a bomb would go off in Dublin" unless the Irish government assumed the bonded debt of the private Irish banks, adding over eight billion euros to Irish state debt, for which the Irish state had no legal obligation.

3. The full story is in my father's memoir, *A Life in Our Times*.

4. In his book *Killing the Host*, Michael Hudson reports that the United States, specifically President Obama and Treasury Secretary Timothy Geithner, in 2011 pressured the Europeans to take a hard line with Greece while extending the debts rather than writing them off. The reason was that US banks had written credit default swaps against a Greek default; by practicing "extend and pretend," the US financial gamblers were saved from a massive payout, while the Greek taxpayer and pensioner was crushed.

5. Internal IMF documents from May 2010 that came into the possession of the Greek Parliament Commission on the Debt confirm these points.

6. Holland was by then and is still teaching at the University of Coimbra, Portugal.

7. Papandreou had decided to put the austerity regime to a vote of the Greek people. For this temerity he was summoned to Cannes by Angela Merkel and Nicolas Sarkozy; the referendum was canceled and Papandreou was destroyed.

8. My contribution to the *Modest Proposal* turned on a proposal for food stamps and school lunches to deal with a growing problem of hunger, especially among children. One of the first acts of the SYRIZA government, providing a debit card worth two hundred euros a month for food in the neediest cases, was built on this idea. The creditors complained hotly.

9. On the return to Athens with Yanis, as he drove in from the airport a motorcyclist roared up alongside in the manner (I thought) of a Mossad man approaching an Iranian physicist. But it was only to lean in and ask, "Are you optimistic"?

10. The jacket actually belonged to the Greek ambassador in Paris, as Yanis had left his own suitcase in a taxi on the way to the airport in Athens. Stratou, then still in Austin, disapproved, and in my baggage I carried over to Athens a suitable cashmere coat. The taxi driver returned the lost suitcase in due course. Eleven Downing Street is the official residence of the Chancellor of the Exchequer.

11. This incident might have come a day later.

12. The finance ministry did pick up some expenses, including hotel bills and some travel costs inside Europe, as well as paying a modest per diem. These were fully disclosed in the ministry's public records.

13. Given the reputation that the Varoufakis ministry had for talking too much, it was a bit of professional pleasure to reveal that we could also keep a secret.

14. In December 2014 the Samaras government was offered a six-month extension of the program, but in view of its likely election loss it asked for, and received, an extension of only two months, thus setting up its successor for an early crisis. George Papandreou had by then been deposed as leader of PASOK, which passed under the hand of Evangelos Venizelos, Papandreou's former deputy prime minister.

15. And actually, for reasons that were never entirely clear, the IMF had adopted a standard that the ratio should be driven down to about 120 percent by a given year (2020, if memory serves), as its criterion of restored market access. There is no evidence that actual markets were consulted on the point; rumor had it that the number was copied from some earlier Italian experience.

16. To counter this on one occasion I leaked a Greek position paper to the *Financial Times*. However, I had misread Yanis's intentions on the matter; he was surprised and reacted furiously against the supposed source somewhere

among the creditor institutions. I confessed, sheepishly. Fortunately the *FT* story on the matter was a good one.

17. One of the nastier episodes concerned a film clip mounted on an otherwise amusing music video by a German comedy team, which showed Yanis making a vulgar finger gesture at a conference in Zagreb two years earlier, in reference to debt payments to Germany. The stink over the "stinke-finger" went on for days and days. Whether Yanis actually made the fleeting gesture or not remains disputed—he has no memory of it, although I have since encountered a credible eyewitness who says he did. But of course the matter was utterly unimportant.

18. Yanis was, however, able to counteract the claim that he had "lost it" at Riga, by circulating audio, recorded on his cell phone, of his own interventions privately to his fellow cabinet members. The fact that he had made such a recording, although perfectly within his rights, caused another kerfuffle in the press.

19. Euclid Tsakalotos is an English-born and -bred Greek, educated at Eton and Oxford, who had been (unlike Yanis) a stalwart of SYRIZA from its beginnings. He was deputy foreign minister for international economic affairs in the January government and would replace Yanis as finance minister in July.

20. In the United States Phil Angelides, former treasurer of the state of California and former chairman of the Financial Crisis Inquiry Commission, played an especially active role. Support also came from the Hellenic Caucus of the US Congress, from Michael Dukakis, and from other leading figures.

21. So far as I was able to learn, the US banking sector was by 2015 little exposed to Greek risk, so the concerns and pressures that drove US policy in 2011 no longer applied.

TWO
Europe's Crisis: Thinking It Through to the End

1. This would be the then-new Greek government of George Papandreou, elected in October 2009. The emergency was the collapse of the Greek budget position and access to the credit markets that followed immediately.

2. Organization for Economic Cooperation and Development, an international body consisting mainly of the world's wealthy democracies, derived from the Marshall Plan, based in Paris.

3. We learned much later that the IMF contribution—which at thirty-two times Greece's quota or ownership share in the IMF was the largest, in relation to quota, in history—had been pushed through by the managing director, Dominique Strauss-Kahn, over the objections of some staff and outside di-

rectors. See the introduction for a brief discussion of Strauss-Kahn's motives. The testimony of the French economist Philippe Legrain to the Greek parliamentary commission on the debt gave additional damning details.

4. Kunibert Raffer is a distinguished trade and development economist at the University of Vienna, and a close student of international debt issues.

5. Five years later, the European superstate remains far out of reach, and it has become clear that if one should be created, it could never have the progressive policy characteristics of the New Deal.

THREE
Greece and the European Project

1. William Isaac, chairman of the Federal Deposit Insurance Corporation under Reagan, confirmed the existence of this plan to me personally in September 2008.

2. At press time in 2016 refugees from Syria—from violence as well as economic collapse—are giving the Europeans a foretaste of mass population movements.

3. These ideas were being framed, at that time, as part of the Varoufakis-Holland *Modest Proposal*. I would join as a coauthor two years later.

FOUR
A Question of Moral Responsibility

1. The debt restructuring foreseen here came about in 2012, although too little and too late.

2. The population cited was incorrect: the actual population of Greece is on the order of 10.8 million.

3. In the diktat of 2015 the secret plan was exposed to plain view, with a privatization fund that was supposed to contain fifty billion euros of Greek public assets, one difficulty being that assets on that scale do not actually exist.

4. Jóse Manuel Barroso was president of the European Commission; Jean-Claude Trichet was president of the European Central Bank; Mario Draghi is Trichet's successor.

5. This and all other quotations from Keynes in this book come from *The Economic Consequences of the Peace*.

FIVE

Neither Austerity nor Growth:
Solidarity *Is Europe's Only Hope*

1. This was a conference of the Institute for New Economic Thinking (INET), which I attended in Berlin in April, 2012.

2. The important recent work of Clara Elisabetta Mattei documents the close links between the ideology of austerity and the development of Italian fascism in the 1920s. I first came across this work, which has not yet been published, in the summer of 2015.

SIX

The Victory of SYRIZA *Is Not*
Against American Interests

1. On June 11, 2013, the Greek government abruptly shut the state television and radio service, ERT, leaving Greeks with no media not directly controlled by private oligarchs or the Orthodox Church.

2. Antonio Samaras, leader of New Democracy, was by this time prime minister, having replaced the "technocratic" administration of Lucas Papademos in 2012.

3. This idea was my central contribution to the *Modest Proposal*, and a version was implemented as the first economic action of the SYRIZA government, providing a 200-euro monthly food supplement to the neediest Greeks. The program has so far survived into the 2015 memorandum, and Yanis Varoufakis generously gave me a word of credit for it on his blog in July.

SEVEN

The United States and Europe: What Is Going On?

1. Olivier Blanchard and Justin Wolfers, "The Role of Shocks and Institutions in the Rise of European Unemployment: The Aggregate Evidence," National Bureau of Economic Research Working Paper 7282, August 1999.

2. The Hartz reforms were a program of labor market liberalization and deregulation, including the creation of "mini-jobs," introduced in Germany pursuant to the work of a commission in the early 2000s.

3. Matteo Renzi became prime minister of Italy in February 2014.

EIGHT
The Greek Hope

1. Seibert is state secretary, head of the Press and Information Office, and spokesman for the German government. The annual meetings of the World Economic Forum, an elite conclave, are held at Davos, Switzerland.
2. In the elections of January 25, 2015, SYRIZA won 149 of 300 seats in the Greek Parliament.

NINE
A Message to Sarah Raskin

1. Actually, the finance minister's office is on the sixth floor of the ministry. Architectural details were not my principal concern at that moment.

TEN
A Comment on the Way Forward

1. The reference is to the first mission of the new government to the Eurogroup and European Council, which began on February 11, 2015, and lasted about a week, culminating in the interim agreement of February 20, 2015, that extended the loan agreement until the end of July.

ELEVEN
America Must Rally to Greece

1. The reference date is February 19, 2015. On the following day, an interim agreement was reached.
2. Slight exaggeration here in the GDP loss: The usual estimate is about a quarter of GDP lost from 2009 to 2014.
3. Technically, the ECB withdrew a waiver that had permitted Greek banks to rediscount low-rated Greek government bonds directly with the ECB. The effect was to force the banks onto a different and more costly facility, emergency liquidity assistance, over which the ECB exercised direct and regular quantitative control. And the effect of that was to deepen anxieties about the stability of the Greek banks and to foster ongoing withdrawals, especially of international credit lines.
4. In the elections of October 2015, Portugal's conservative government lost its majority, and the subsequent formation of an anti-austerity alliance between

the Socialists, Communists, and Left Bloc demonstrated that the strategy of intimidating other European voters with the Greek example did not work.

5. A currency swap would have been, of course, a measure to consider post–exit from the euro. I was attempting here to drop a calculated hint.

6. In the end, the US government offered a number of supportive words, but mixed messages and no practical financial help.

TWELVE
Reading The Greek Deal Correctly

1. The reference date is February 20, 2015.

2. John Cassidy, "How Greece Got Outmaneuvered," *New Yorker*, February 20, 2015.

3. I confess it was I who spotted the word in the boiler room with the Greek team at the European Commission, and sang out, to the tune of the *Internationale*, "We shall build, on a new arrangement . . ."

4. In the end, improbably, the Greek government both capitulated and survived. How much the larger European landscape has changed remains, for the present, an open question.

THIRTEEN
A Great German Greek Grexit Game?

1. Tony Curzon Price, "The Greek Game: Dominance or Chicken, Fear or Reason?" openEconomy, March 8, 2015; Frances Coppola, "High-Stakes European Poker: A Reply to Curzon Price," openDemocracy, March 7, 2015. These are the dates given on the Web; why the Curzon Price piece postdates the reply is an unexplained mystery.

2. "Grexit" is an odious Goldman-Sachs coinage for Greek exit from the euro. I avoid it wherever possible.

3. This piece, and probably this paragraph, represented the high point of my optimism, such as it was, that the negotiations might possibly yield an acceptable deal. It was downhill from the next paragraph on.

FOURTEEN
The Political Level

1. There were installments due to the IMF in mid-March; the Greeks felt it important to meet these payment deadlines so as not to be declared in default on a wide range of other debts.

FIFTEEN

A Report from Athens

1. Thank you Philippe [Pochet, chair of the European Trade Union Institute]. I am very happy to be here. And as you say, something is happening in Europe. But what, exactly? That is the question.

2. "Podemos" is Spanish for "Yes, we can," and also the name of the then-rising Left political party, headed by Pablo Iglesias, and growing out of the "Indignados" movement against austerity in Spain.

3. The reference was to a meeting held between Chancellor Merkel and Prime Minister Tsipras, at her invitation. My slight optimism was unfounded.

4. The alleged gesture came (or perhaps didn't) during a 2013 talk to the "Subversive Festival" in Zagreb, and was disseminated at the end of a music video entitled "V for Varoufakis," prepared and aired by a German comedy team. The uproar preoccupied the German and Greek press for many days— Greek TV took to running split-screen images, half current news and half a still from the video showing Yanis with the middle finger raised. Eventually the attacks collapsed under the weight of the farce that they were.

5. Truth is on the march and nothing can stop it. Thank you.

SIXTEEN

Does Europe Need Debt Relief?

1. A series of conferences on the international financial crisis were organized in 1986 under the aegis of Senator Bill Bradley and Representative Jack Kemp; the actual work was done by the late Richard Medley, a former aide to Senate Minority Leader Robert Byrd and a close friend since graduate school, and by David Smick, a former Kemp staffer who continues as the editor of the *International Economy*. I had been responsible for introducing Medley to the staff of the US Congress, an achievement of some chutzpah considering the man's views. He went on to help George Soros break the British pound in 1992, and then, having made his first $50 million, finished his PhD before going on to a financial and consulting career.

2. The Eurogroup is the name given to the quasi-formal, regular meetings of the Eurozone's nineteen finance ministers, a dreary ritual known for wasting time and accomplishing little. Yanis Varoufakis had to endure a large number of these meetings.

3. Brady bonds, named after George H. W. Bush's treasury secretary Nicholas Brady, were bonds denominated in dollars that were issued to reduce the debt burden of Latin American countries affected by the debt crisis of the early 1980s.

SEVENTEEN
SEVENTEEN
Long-Term Strategy Through a Realistic Lens

1. The New Development Model was one of our efforts to present a coherent economic plan to the European partners; a copy is available on Yanis Varoufakis's blog at www.yanisvaroufakis.eu.

2. Economists' shorthand. By "price rigidity" I meant the possibility that a newly devalued drachma would not reduce Greece's prices in relation to its competitors, because key sectors might continue to set their prices in euros. By "demand inelasticity" I meant to convey the possibility that reduced prices might not increase volumes sold.

3. See the definition of debt deflation in the introduction.

4. A swap line is an arrangement between central banks to exchange each other's money at a given rate. In 2008–2009 the Federal Reserve provided hundreds of billions of dollars in exchange for euros, Swiss francs, Korean won, and Mexican pesos, stabilizing those currencies in the crisis.

5. Argentina in the wake of the 2002 crisis instituted a modest but successful scheme under which the state served as employer of last resort; the scheme atrophied over time as the Argentine economy recovered.

EIGHTEEN
Strategic Options

1. The reference is to a payment made in May to the IMF that avoided a default at that moment. In September the press reported what had happened: the president of the Bank of Greece, Yannis Stournaris, had contacted the Greek executive director at the IMF and arranged for the payment to be made against $700 million in special drawing rights that were in the Greek account at the IMF. The finance ministry was not informed and, having braced for a default, we were taken by surprise.

2. Here, as elsewhere in these texts, I'm reminded of how clear the timeline was to us, all the way through.

NINETEEN
A Further Message to Sarah Raskin

1. Emergency liquidity assistance was the financial lifeline from the European Central Bank to the Greek banks, which drew on it to cash out the deposits that were being withdrawn from the Greek banking system. Capping the ELA could have precipitated a panic; withdrawing it would mean that the

ECB could seize the remaining Greek bank deposits and shut down the Greek banking system.

2. My point, here and in other communications with US officials, is that Greece was already under a swap line with the Federal Reserve, since Greece was in the euro and such a line exists with the European Central Bank. Therefore, if Greece were to exit the euro, continuity of US policy would consist in backstopping the drachma with a separate swap line. This argument got little traction and I fell back on urging that the Fed persuade the ECB to backstop the drachma, thus taking an indirect route. There was unfortunately not much chance that would work either.

TWENTY
The Greek Drama and Democracy in Europe

1. The reference is to the "memorandum of understanding" that underpinned the 2014 extension of the financing arrangement between Greece and its creditors.
2. No to a two-speed Europe.
3. The correct quotation is: "Il n'y a point besoin d'espérer pour entreprendre, ni de réussir pour persévérer"—There is no need to hope before trying, nor to succeed in order to persevere.

TWENTY-ONE
Notes on the Meeting . . .

1. Following a previous Varoufakis-Schäuble meeting at which the possibility of exit was broached, Varoufakis reported to Tsipras, who raised the question directly with Merkel; the chancellor responded that if her finance minister brought it up again, she wanted to know. This put the Greek government in the curious position of being brought, after a fashion, into the internal communications of the German government.
2. The Securities Market Program (SMP) was an ECB initiative under Jean-Claude Trichet to purchase government bonds on the open market, thereby supporting their price and sparing the private holders of those bonds, mostly banks, the losses that they would have otherwise suffered when Greek debt was restructured in 2012. The European Stability Mechanism (ESM) is a permanent agency created in 2012 to lend to states and for bank recapitalizations in the Eurozone.

TWENTY-TWO
What Is Reform? The Strange Case of Greece and Europe

1. As described in the previous piece, on June 8, 2015, Yanis and I traveled to Berlin for a private meeting with the German finance minister, Wolfgang Schäuble, followed by a public lecture. It was a last throw, but there was nothing to be had.

TWENTY-FOUR
Bad Faith

1. IMF Managing Director Christine Lagarde, formerly the French finance minister.

TWENTY-FIVE
Only the "No" Can Save the Euro

1. In early June, Greece had exercised an option to "bundle" its June payments to the IMF into a single payment due on June 30, thus buying a bit of time before falling into arrears to the Fund. In the event, the June 30 payment was not made, and Greece did slip into arrears at that point. The arrears were not cleared until the government capitulated and the third memorandum was signed.

2. A sly remark on my part, since at this point, I was the one making the preparations and keeping the secret.

TWENTY-SEVEN
What Is the Matter With Europe?

1. My reference here was to the January elections and the strong support given to the government through the spring. I did not at this moment yet know the astonishing outcome of the referendum.

TWENTY-EIGHT
Exit Made Easy

1. The SWIFT/IBAN codes are used to identify individual banks and accounts for the purpose of making interbank and international payments.

2. See the explanation on pages 192–193.

3. To be fair, there was and is no guarantee of this, and uncertainty over whether the exchange rate could be defended was a major factor in the thinking of the prime minister.

THIRTY-TWO
Note to the Guardian

1. "Yanis Varoufakis May Face Criminal Charges over Greek Currency Plan," *Guardian*, July 29, 2015.

THIRTY-THREE
Death Spiral Ahead?

1. In the elections held on September 20, 2015, the 62 percent had no viable options. SYRIZA had become committed to implementation of the memorandum, while the pro-drachma Left Platform, reconstituted as the new party Popular Unity, did not have leadership that provided a credible alternative to SYRIZA.

THIRTY-FOUR
The Future of Europe

1. Giuseppe Guarino, "The Truth About Europe and the Euro: An Essay," available at http://www.giuseppeguarino.it/pubblicazioni/.

THIRTY-SIX
Back to Square Zero

1. See "Diary: In Athens," July 30, 2015.

THIRTY-SEVEN
A Final Word

1. My paternal grandfather, William Archibald Galbraith, was Liberal Party chief in the riding of Elgin West, Southern Ontario, in the 1920s and 1930s. That night, after my speech, word came of the political developments in Por-

tugal, where the anti-austerity left had forged a coalition capable of holding a majority in the Portuguese parliament. This development fanned the flames of revolt in Europe and provoked a major political crisis in Portugal, when the conservative president, Cavaco Silva, initially refused to allow the Left to form a government.

2. The Spanish translation of "yes, we can" is, of course, "Podemos."

APPENDIX

A Summary of Plan X

1. Legal advice persuaded us that the second course of action—putting the Bank of Greece into bankruptcy rather than nationalizing it outright, and then immediately replacing the functions with a new legal entity—a New Bank of Greece—was preferable because it would block the claim of the European Central Bank for any immediate repayment of the emergency liquidity assistance.

2. The need to reprogram bank accounts and payments systems and the impossibility of achieving this in a short period of time was a major headache, and we did not solve that problem with the information at hand. I am now convinced that the way to do it would be to leave existing euro bank accounts intact, but blocked with capital controls from either transfer abroad or withdrawal from the Greek banking system except via paper drachma. These accounts would then automatically revalue to the value of the New Drachma and the reprogramming could be done as a back office matter over months, without affecting electronic payments within Greece, which could proceed normally from the beginning.

3. We examined the historical experience with scrip in some detail; that was the subject of a separate memorandum.

4. This was precautionary; we did not have available an inventory of Greek gold reserves, and to request such information from the Bank of Greece—a private entity controlled by the political opposition—would have been too risky.

5. Greek government bonds.

6. I borrowed this idea from the American economist Dean Baker.